I0090041

Radical Healing

*Hypnosis Practitioner's Guide to Harnessing the
Healing Power of the Educational Pre-Talk*

Wendie Webber

Radical Healing: *Hypnosis Practitioner's Guide to Harnessing the Healing Power of the Educational Pre-Talk*

Wendie Webber

Copyright © 2021 Wendie Webber
All Rights Reserved.

All rights reserved. No part of this publication may be reproduced, distributed, or transmitted in any form or by any means, including photocopying, recording, or other electronic or mechanical methods without the prior written permission from the author, except in the case of brief quotations embodied in critical reviews and certain non-commercial uses permitted by copyright law.

The information given in this book should not be treated as a substitute for professional medical advice; always consult a medical practitioner. Any use of information in this book is at the reader's discretion and risk. Neither the author nor the publisher can be held responsible for any loss, claim, or damage arising out of use, or misuse, of the suggestions made, the failure to take medical advice, or for any material on third-party websites.

ISBN Print Book: 978-1-7774121-6-6

TABLE OF CONTENTS

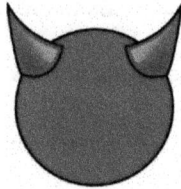

WHY READ THIS BOOK

traveler comes upon a large group of villagers gathered at the river. Finding this curious, the traveler moves in for a closer look. "What's happening?" he asks. One of the villagers replies frantically, "Someone is throwing babies into the river! We're trying to rescue them!" The traveler looks at the situation. He observes that the problem seems to be increasing. As the number of babies floating down the river continues to grow, so does the crowd at the river as more and more villagers are called in to join in the efforts to save the babies.

The traveler considers the situation carefully, then turns to resume his journey on the path along the river. Surprised, the villager calls after him, "Where are you going? Aren't you going to help?" The traveler smiles and responds, "Yes. I'm going upstream to find out who's throwing them in."

Clients are going to come to you with all kinds of problems. They might be dealing with physical symptoms such as an ache, pain, or trouble sleeping. They may be struggling with unwanted behavior, low self-esteem, or chronic negative thinking. But symptoms, like babies floating down the river, are not the problem.

Symptoms may serve to motivate a person to seek help, but they are seldom the whole problem. When a person thinks, or feels, or acts in ways that they don't like, it's because their Conscious Mind doesn't know what the real problem is. As a result, it can't fix it. All the Conscious Mind can do is come up with reasons, excuses, and ways to avoid the perceived problem.

Unfortunately, these strategies tend to make things worse. This is why problems tend to get worse over time. It's because the Conscious Mind just doesn't have the whole Story. As a hypnosis practitioner, you are uniquely qualified to gain access to that Story. You can help a client to identify the real problem and can come up with a better solution. But to do that, you need a Contract.

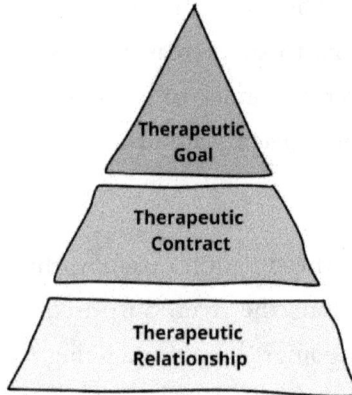

The Contract

The Therapeutic Contract is an agreement between you and your client. This contract is based on the Therapeutic Relationship and serves the purpose of achieving the client's Therapeutic Goal.

The Therapeutic Contract allows you to do your job by laying the foundation for the work you and the client will do together. This begins by establishing the Therapeutic Relationship. The process of establishing the Therapeutic Relationship begins long before the client's first session. It begins with your first contact with the client.

The Therapeutic Contract permits you to guide the healing process. But to be binding, this contract requires informed consent. This is the purpose of your educational pre-talk. It's to prepare your client to be an active participant in their healing.

Do you promote yourself and your services?

All marketing is an educational pre-talk. Regardless of the medium, you use to promote your services, it's all about how you can help. It might be by way of your website, on social media, or by attending a social event. It might be through print advertising or a presentation you give. But everything you do to promote yourself and your services is a pre-talk about what you do and how you can help a person put an end to the pain of a problem they've been struggling with. That's what people are looking for—a solution to a problem.

The Contract associated with your marketing material is called a Call to Action. The Call to Action tells a person interested in your services what to do next. What do you want the person to do next? You want them to pick up the phone and call you, right? That's a Contract!

Do you field calls about your services?

When a person picks up a phone to call you, your initial conversation with the caller is a pre-talk. This pre-talk aims to make it safe for the person to commit to the first session. To do that, they need to feel that they can trust you. For many people, the Subconscious is a dark and scary place filled with unknowns. They do not want to go there! You need them to trust you to guide them through uncharted waters. The Contract associated with the first call is committing to the first session. That's the next logical step.

Do you educate your clients about the process?

The purpose of educating the client in the first session is to remove fears and misconceptions about the process. But Regression Hypnotherapy is not a passive process. You're not merely inducing hypnosis and delivering a few suggestions. You're guiding a person to face painful, past experiences so they can resolve them for good. But to do this requires the client's participation.

To be successful, the client must be prepared to allow uncomfortable memories and emotions to be a part of the process. You can't merely suggest an emotion away.[1] You need to go upstream to find out what's causing the problem. To do this, you need the client's permission. For this reason, Regression Hypnotherapy requires a much more comprehensive educational pretalk.

Educating the client about the healing process allows them to make an informed decision to let you guide the healing process. The Contract for Regression Hypnotherapy permits you to guide the therapeutic process while making the client responsible for the results.

---

[1] Regression to Cause Hypnotherapy does not focus on removing or managing symptoms. If you were taught to amputate a feeling, stuff it in a box, or banish it from consciousness, stop. That's just asking for trouble!

The Devil's Therapy

The Devil's Therapy: Hypnosis Practitioner's Essential Guide to Effective Regression Hypnotherapy provides the theoretical foundation you need to confidently facilitate client-centered healing programs. Most importantly, it answers the question, "Why do we do what we do when we do it?"

Ditch the Script: Get Everything You Need from the Client for Successful Hypnotherapy and Set Up to Wrap Up with Results shows you how to break free of "scripnotism" by revealing simple strategies you can use to set up for effective Regression Hypnotherapy.

Radical Healing: Hypnosis Practitioner's Guide to Harnessing the Healing Power of the Educational Pre-talk provides the keys to preparing your clients to be successful working with you by making them an active participant in their own healing.

If you're trained in Regression Hypnotherapy . . .

If you've ever been asked what you do . . .

If you've ever had to give a talk on hypnotherapy . . .

If you want to empower yourself by empowering your clients . . .

This book is for you.

In Chapter 1, we'll look at how promoting yourself and your services is an educational pre-talk designed to establish a contract.

In Chapter 2, we'll look at how to educate a prospective client in a way that establishes a contract for the first session.

In Chapter 3, we'll dive into the main component for educating a client in readiness for Regression to Cause Therapeutic Hypnosis—your Mind Model.

In Chapter 4, we'll look at how to establish a contract that allows hypnosis by addressing common misconceptions which can generate unnecessary resistance to being hypnotized.

In Chapter 5, we'll explore the mind-body connection and how stress is a major contributor to many of the issues clients typically seek out your help in resolving. *The Devil's Therapy* is a body-centered approach to healing with the Mind.

In Chapter 6, we'll look at how symptoms are not the problem, what the real problem is, and how to make the client responsible for the results.

In Chapter 7, you'll learn the secret to rapid relief and how to use it during your educational pre-talk to teach your client how to work with you in regression sessions successfully.

In Chapter 8, we'll look at establishing a binding Contract for Regression Hypnotherapy and test it using the three Fs.

You'll also find three additional bonus chapters from professionals in the field of Regression Hypnotherapy.

In Chapter 9, Barbara Scholl, creator of Hypno-Kids, will share valuable insights on educating parents and teenagers for effective Therapeutic Hypnosis.

In Chapter 10, Scott Allerton of Sydney Integrative Hypnotherapy offers tips on how to get rid of unnecessary resistance by using brain science to educate your more analytical or science-minded clients.

In Chapter 11, Emotional Intelligence Development Specialist and Morpho-psychologist Daniel Ghanimé address the unique needs of palliative clients and educate them to prepare them for the healing process.

Ready to get started?

Read on.

radical

1. *of, relating to, or* **proceeding from a root**

2. *of, or relating to, the origin:* FUNDAMENTAL

3. *very different from the usual or traditional:* EXTREME

4. *slang:* EXCELLENT, COOL

Origin: Middle English, from Late Latin radicalis, *from Latin* radic-, radix *root — more at root*

—————— ⧜ ——————

heal

1. *a: to make free from injury or disease:* **to make sound or whole**
   b: to make well again: to restore to health

2. *a: to cause (an undesirable condition) to be overcome: MEND*
   b: to patch up or correct (a breach or division)

3. *: to restore to original purity or integrity*
   Origin: Old English hǽlan *(in the sense 'restore to sound health'), of Germanic origin; related to Dutch* heelen *and German* heilen, *also to make whole.*

~ **Merriam-Webster Dictionary**

CHAPTER 1:
Contract the Call

All marketing is essentially a pre-talk. Whether in person, online, or in print, your marketing material is educating a person about who you can help and how you can help them get rid of a depressing, painful problem. That's all anyone is interested in—can you help them get free of the pain of the problem?

Everybody has a frustrating problem that they would love to be free of. And you may just be the answer they've been looking for. But they won't realize this if they don't pick up the phone to call you. If you can grab their attention by speaking to the problem they're struggling with, they may be intrigued enough to call you. That's all you need because marketing isn't about booking the session. It's about getting the right person to call you.

Who? What? How?

The purpose of your marketing pre-talk is to invite a person to learn more about how you can help them. This begins with identifying who your ideal client is. Who is your ideal client? What one specific problem do they have that you understand so well? What do you know that they don't know? How can you transform their life for the better?

What makes you the best choice for this person? Answering these three questions—Who? What? How?—gives you everything you need to create an educational pre-talk to promote yourself and your services in a way that attracts more callers.

Who is your ideal client?

Think about the one you just *love* to work with. Who comes to mind when you think of your dream client? You know, the one person that you wish *all* your clients were like? Who is that one person who is such an ideal match for you that you wish you could just clone them? That's your ideal client.

What's their problem?

The way to get a person to call you is to speak directly to the pain of the problem they're struggling with. That's the only thing they care about. Think about the emotional pain of the problem. Emotion is what motivates a person to take action. Think about the shame, the guilt, the fear, the frustration, the anger this problem has been causing them. What painful problem is your ideal client struggling with? What's been keeping them awake at night? Speak to that!

How can you help?

How are you the perfect solution for a person who is struggling with this specific problem? How can you help them to achieve their desired outcome? In other words, how are you the answer they've been looking for? Not the hypnosis. YOU.

Don't talk about hypnosis. Most people don't care about hypnosis. People care about their health, wealth, happiness, work, relationships, children, and success. Talk about that and how you help your clients to achieve their desired goals.

Be specific.

What's one specific issue that you'd love to help your ideal client to overcome? What issue would you most love to work with? What problem has the most heart for you? What problem are you most knowledgeable about? What are you most interested in learning more about?

What does a person who is struggling with that painful problem want so much that they would gladly pay money to get it? The relief? The control? The freedom?

How are you uniquely qualified to help this person?

Put the answers to these questions together, and you have everything you need to craft your marketing pre-talk by formulating a Who-What-How statement. For example,

> "I help hypnosis practitioners develop their expertise at facilitating Regression to Cause Hypnotherapy so they can feel confident working with the more complex issues."

WHO? Hypnosis practitioners.

WHAT? The problem of lack of confidence working with more complex issues.

HOW? By developing their expertise at facilitating Regression-to-Cause Therapeutic Hypnosis.

Here are a few more examples of Who-What-How statements:

"I help women who are emotional over-eaters get back in control of their eating habits so that they can get slim and trim and feel good about themselves."

"I help men who are going through a painful marriage breakup feel worthy of love again."

"I help teenagers become academic rock-stars by improving their study skills and helping them overcome test anxiety!"

"I help kids, who have a problem with bedwetting, wake to a dry bed every morning so that they can feel good about themselves, and their parents can have peace of mind (and finally get a good night's sleep!)."

Okay, maybe these Who-What-How statements don't speak specifically to what you care most about or want to do. It's up to you to formulate your own Who-What-How statement.

Your Who-What-How statement will support you in growing a referral-based healing practice. You do it by delivering on your promise of results. Do that, and people will gladly pay you a premium fee for your services. As you grow your reputation as a trusted guide and expert healer, your many satisfied clients will come back to work on other issues with you. Not only that, but they'll also send you their friends and family members. They'll even recommend you to strangers. It all begins with answering those three simple questions.

1. Who do you help?
2. What do you help them with?
3. How can they benefit from working with you?

Presentations

Do you give presentations or information talks? If you educate your audience about what you do, that's a pre-talk! Giving a talk is a great way to promote yourself and your services. The trick is to think of your group as one person with a **specific** problem. Then, speak directly to how they are struggling with the problem and how you can help them put an end to the pain it's been causing them—physically, mentally, or emotionally.

The list of issues that you can give a talk on is endless. For example, smoking, weight loss, painless childbirth, pain management, life purpose, past lives, sports performance, academic performance. Other issues that hypnosis can help resolve include:

- Chronic stress
- Childhood trauma
- Bereavement
- Clarity or direction in life
- Relationship issues
- Money issues
- Goal achievement
- Troublesome dreams
- Blocks to creativity
- Control
- Self-confidence
- Self-esteem
- Fears and phobias
- Procrastination
- Test anxiety
- People-pleasing
- Depression

- Sleep problems

The list goes on.

Whatever you choose to give a talk on, your educational pre-talk should answer those three questions. Who do you help? What do you help them with? How can you help? Who is your ideal client?

Your talk should demonstrate your knowledge of your chosen topic. Show that you understand the pain of the problem and that you care. Share a few examples of how you have helped others with this problem. Address common misconceptions about hypnosis. Answer questions. Then, talk about your unique approach.

- What specific issues do you most love to work with?
- How can hypnosis make it easier to achieve a specific goal?
- What are the most common misconceptions about hypnosis?
- What makes your approach different or unique?
- How can you quickly give your audience a rewarding experience to prove that you might be the answer they've been looking for?
- What's the next logical step?

Always end with a Call to Action. What do you want them to do next? Call you, right? Think of an incentive you can offer folks to take action, right way. Make it easy and low risk. For example, you could offer a free consultation to discuss their issue privately, either by phone or in your office.[2]

---

[2] You can learn more low-cost strategies for promoting yourself in the Hypnosis Practice Client Attraction System at www.tribeofhealers.com

The Call to Action

Remember, marketing is all about the call. The purpose of your marketing efforts is not to sell the session. It's to get a person to pick up the phone and call you. You do that by providing sufficient information to enable a person to pre-qualify themselves. What a prospective client wants to know is:

1. Are you the right therapist for them?
2. Have you helped others with the same problem as they have?

If you have helped others get rid of the same problem, they're going to want to learn more. That's when they'll pick up the phone and call you. This is where testimonials can help you to get more calls. Testimonials are like mini pre-talks. What makes them so valuable is that they are being delivered by satisfied clients who enthusiastically recommend you to others. This provides proof to the reader that it's worth it for them to call you to learn more. That's what you want.

What your ideal client wants to know is—What happened?

- What changed as a result of working with you?
- What was it like working with you?
- What surprised your client about the process?
- Were they apprehensive about the process to begin with? If so, how did this change?
- How is your approach uniquely different from other methods they tried?
- How did your satisfied client benefit from the process?
- What unexpected side benefits did they enjoy as a result of the process?

The Initial Conversation

Your first contact with a prospective new client might be by telephone, Zoom, Skype, or in person. But the purpose of this initial conversation is not to sell the session. It's to build rapport, remove fears and misconceptions about the healing process, and qualify your client. Qualifying your clients is essential to your success simply because you cannot be all things to all people[3].

If you want to get consistent results, you need to be realistic. Don't try to take on more than you're ready for. You'll just end up with problems you don't need. To stay in your groove, you need to assess whether the caller is the right client for you. While you're qualifying a prospective client, you can address any fears or misconceptions they might have about hypnosis and Regression Hypnotherapy.

Common misconceptions about hypnosis can usually be resolved before the client comes in for their first session. The problem is that most people don't turn to hypnosis first. It's usually not until they have tried everything else that they decide to "try" hypnosis. By the time they decide to pick up the phone to call you, they're scared and frustrated and depressed, which can make them apprehensive about committing to the process. That's understandable.

Doubts & Concerns

When a prospective client expresses doubts and concerns about the process, keep them focused on the problem. That's why they called you. Make it safe for them to be open and honest with you about what

---

[3] You can learn more in *Ditch the Script: Get Everything You Need from the Client for Successful Hypnotherapy and Set Up to Wrap Up with Results.*

they've been dealing with. The longer they talk with you, the more invested they become in what you can offer them.

If they've tried everything else and nothing has worked, listen. Show that you care. Validate how they feel. Then find out what, specifically, they're concerned about. Teach them how your approach is different. For example, if you're dealing with a behavior issue, say,

> "Most people try to use willpower. You know how long that lasts—about thirty seconds. This is different."

Help your prospective client to feel smart for having made the important decision to take the first step by calling you. Then find out what motivated them to take that action. For example,

> "You know yourself. You know what you've been through and what got you here. Why did you decide you need a hypnotherapist to help you?"

No Regression!

What if a caller is resistant to Regression Hypnosis because the feelings are too intense? What if they don't want to revisit past events or confront their feelings? What if the caller says, "No regression!"? Realize that, just as people have fears and misconceptions about hypnosis, they have fears and misconceptions about regression. Most of these fears have to do with being overwhelmed, losing control, or revealing some deep, dark secret.

Whatever the objection might be, interrupt the pattern. Smile and say, "Yes, I hear that a lot." Then, shift their attention away from what they don't want and onto what they do want—the benefits of change.

For example, if the client reveals a fear of being overwhelmed or out of control to their feelings, say,

> "You're already out of control. That's why you're here. I'm here to put you in control."

If they're afraid of revealing some deep, dark secrets, say,

> "You don't have to share anything you don't want to share. I don't need to hear all the details. The only thing we're interested in is the feeling so that we can change it."

Sometimes, the person will consciously recall traumatic experiences that they flat-out do not want to revisit. What they don't realize is that the problem *now* is not what happened *then*. The problem *now* is one of avoidance. Don't reinforce this habituated pattern by trying to negotiate with the client. Remember, if the client knew how to resolve the problem, they wouldn't need you. You cannot let the client dictate the therapy and expect to be successful. For example, if they don't want to revisit painful events from the past, say,

> "I get that. But look at what you've been dealing with! You've been living in hell!"

If you're dealing with a physical or emotional problem, say,

> "Everything out there is focused on the symptoms. This is different. The reason we can get such amazing results is that the focus is finding the root. We want to dig down, find out what's causing the symptoms, so we can pull out the roots. That way, there's nothing left to generate the problem. Do that, and you can begin to experience extraordinary change for the better in your life."

Most other approaches encourage avoidance. But when it comes to working with emotional issues, avoidance is the problem. Guess where the solution lies? The one place the client hasn't been willing to look. The one place you're telling them that they need to go. Remind your prospective client of everything they've already tried. The reason they still have the problem is because all the stuff they've been trying to avoid is still there, just below the surface. Hold the client accountable for achieving the results. For example,

> "How much is holding onto this problem costing you? If nothing changes, nothing changes, right? To get a different result, you need to be willing to use a different approach. That's where you'll find the healing."

What the client doesn't realize is that they're reliving the same pattern of thoughts, feelings, reactivity, and behavior, over and over, again. Day in and day out, they're at war with the symptoms. That is hell. They already know this. Remind them of how much pain this problem has been causing them. Then offer them a choice. For example,

> "It's up to you. Do you want me to help you relax, or do you want to get rid of the problem for good? Either way is okay with me."

Remember, the client doesn't know how to resolve the problem. *You do.* But to go upstream and locate the cause of the problem, you need the client's permission. Before you book the first session, make sure to establish a Contract that gives you permission to decide on the therapy because you don't just need more clients. You need clients you can be successful with. If a person is unwilling to let you be in charge of the therapeutic process, you can't help them.

Success requires a commitment. The client must be ready to go where you need them to go to get the healing. That's the Contract. If they're not willing to let you guide the process, cut them loose. For example,

> "I don't think this is the best approach for you, at this time. Thanks for your interest."

Summary

Anything you do to market or promote your services is essentially a pre-talk. Whether it's in person, on your website, or by giving a presentation, the purpose of your marketing efforts isn't to try to sell a session. It's to get a person to call you.

You are the answer for a lot more people than you probably realize. But your prospective new client won't realize this if you don't get that initial conversation with them. Your Who-What-How statement helps your ideal client decide to pick up the phone and call you.

Testimonials from satisfied clients are mini pre-talks that speak directly to those who could benefit from your services. If you helped someone with the same problem as your prospective new client, they're going to want to learn more. That's when they'll pick up the phone and call you.

Your initial conversation with a prospective client allows you to qualify your client and establish a Contract that allows you to decide the therapy. This marks the beginning of the Therapeutic Relationship. The next step is to establish a Contract for the first session.

CHAPTER 2:
Contract the First Session

S ome people are going to be nervous about coming to see you for the first time. That's to be expected, especially if they've never experienced hypnosis before. The problem is that human beings naturally fear the unknown. What the client doesn't know about the healing process can result in no-shows. No-shows cost you.

Between the time you book the first appointment and the client actually showing up for their first session, they can get cold feet. They'll talk themselves out of it. Friends and family members will instill doubt. They'll start worrying whether they can be hypnotized or what might be revealed through the process. Some people have performance anxiety. They'll project this fear onto the hypnosis by worrying that they might not do it right or that they can't be hypnotized. These are valid concerns that need to be addressed before the client shows up for their first session.

The biggest mistake, even the pros make, is keeping the first session cloaked in mystery. Seriously, if hypnosis is such a normal, natural, everyday human experience, why the need for secrecy? Even a niggling little fear can get in the way if you don't resolve it ahead of time. But if you can take the client from worrying about what might happen to looking forward to the process, no-shows will be a thing of the past.

What's going to happen?

Use your initial conversation to root out any worries or concerns the client be harboring. Then, get rid of any anticipatory fear by telling the client what's going to happen. Not all the details, of course. Just enough for them to see that it's no big deal. Put the client's mind at ease by educating them about what to expect in that first session. Remove all the fear and mystery and get them looking forward to the benefits of change instead. Then, instead of worrying about what might be revealed or how they might fail, the client will be anticipating success. They'll be curious about what they might learn. This gives you a much more resourceful client to work with when they do arrive. For example,

> "The purpose of the first session is assessment. This session will give me the information I need to design a program that's right for you.

During your initial conversation with a prospective client, get them to imagine what's going to happen in their first session before they even arrive. Get them mentally experiencing being with you, feeling safe and secure. This makes it somewhat familiar. To the Subconscious Mind, familiar means safe. For example,

> "During the session, three things are going to happen. First, we're going to talk. Second, I'm going to teach you what you need to know to be successful working with me. Third, you're going to learn how to relax into hypnosis."

Talk

What's going to happen? First, you're going to talk. Let the client know that you will take the time to get to know them a little better. This lets the client know that you're not just going to dump them into hypnosis. You're going to listen to them. This reassures the Conscious Mind that it will be heard. Let the client know that you will be asking them a lot of questions and that you want to take a history of the problem. This is setting up for the regression work by reinforcing the importance of past experiences and how they might be contributing to the problem.[4]

Teach

What's going to happen? You're going to teach the client what they need to know to be successful working with you. Human beings love to learn. Learning evokes curiosity. Curiosity is a resource state. You're setting your client up to be more resourceful when they show up for their first session. Nice, right? This also helps to remove any performance anxiety the client might still be holding onto while shifting their attention onto the desired results.

Relax

What's going to happen? They're going to learn how to relax. Some people may be a little apprehensive about entering into a state of hypnosis. But everybody is willing to relax. Let the client know that you will guide them through a short process where they will learn how to relax into hypnosis. The keywords here are "short" and "relaxation." Telling the client that the hypnosis session will be short lets them relax

---

[4] You can learn more about how to conduct the intake process for Regression hypnotherapy in *Ditch the Script: Get Everything You Need from the Client for Successful Hypnotherapy and Set Up to Wrap Up with Results.*

about it. This also establishes reasonable expectations for the first session because you sometimes won't have time for more than a short hypnosis session.

Relaxation Hypnosis is ideal for an assessment session because it's slow. This gives you more time to observe the client's responses and teach them how to interact with you during sessions[5]. This will make your job easier when it comes time to start regressing the client into painful events from the past.

Some clients will need more time during the intake process. That's okay. But you still need to do the hypnosis because that's what the client thinks they're paying for. What the client is paying you for is the results. This is the underlying purpose of the first session. It's to prepare the client to be an active participant in the healing process. Preparing your client for the therapeutic work of Regression Hypnosis is a way of empowering the client in readiness for regression. Besides, Relaxation Hypnosis feels good.

By making your client's first experience of hypnosis with you a positive one, you set the tone for future successes. Just make it clear to the client that hypnosis is not relaxation, that you will be *using* relaxation in the first session for a specific reason. It's to teach them how to work with you. This is important because not everyone is able to relax. When it comes time to do the emotional release work, the client will be feeling some uncomfortable feelings like tension and tightness. That's anything *but* relaxed!

[5] Learn more in the Ready for Regression First Session course at tribeofhealers.com

If you don't educate your clients to allow uncomfortable feelings to be a part of the process, the moment they don't feel relaxed, they could decide that they're not in hypnosis. And the moment they start thinking, that brings in the Conscious Mind and its game over. The Conscious Mind has been activated and has the power to block the hypnosis.

The Contract

Once you have informed the client about what's going to happen in the first session—that you're going to talk, you're going to teach them what they need to know, and that you're going to guide them through a short Relaxation Hypnosis session—you can establish an expectation for subsequent sessions. The way to do this is to let the client know that, at the end of the first session, they can decide how they wish to proceed with you. Regression Hypnotherapy is not a single-session approach. It is a client-centered approach guided by the specific needs of each client. For example,

> "At the end of the first session, you can decide how you want to proceed with me. You can continue on a per-session basis, or you can choose to take advantage of a session package, which will save you a few bucks."

This serves two purposes. First, it gets rid of the unrealistic expectation of a one-session miracle. While healing can happen in a heartbeat, it's an unrealistic expectation simply because you can't *make* the client change. You don't have the power. The power is in the Mind of the client. Even when the client is ready, willing, and able to allow healing to happen, even if they really want it in a single session, delivering a one-session miracle requires considerable skill and confidence. If you're just starting, you're probably still figuring things out. Expecting a one-hit-wonder is putting too much pressure on yourself. Set your clients up with realistic expectations, and you'll dramatically improve your success rate right from the start.

Second, the only way to know, for sure, that the issue has been completely resolved is to test the results in the client's daily life. That's where the rubber meets the road. If you don't test, you're going to end up sending people out half-baked. Then, when your one-session miracle fails, and the client experiences a return of symptoms, they'll assume that hypnosis doesn't work. That just hurts all of us.

No matter what happens in a session, you're still going to need a follow-up session. Realize that most people are going to need a process. They don't need you to fix them. They just need you to make it safe enough for them to face the truth of their feelings because those feelings are uncomfortable. It generates resistance. Resistance burns up session time. But the time it takes isn't up to you. It's up to the client. A client-centered approach allows the client whatever time they need to feel safe enough to allow healing to happen.

Baby Steps

When you use your first session as a preliminary assessment system, there's no pressure. For the client, it's just one small commitment to the first session. When you tell them what will happen in their first session, it's a baby step into a known rather than a giant leap into the unknown. The first session also gives you a better idea of what you're dealing with. This can help you to identify how best to proceed with the client. For example, some clients will need ego-strengthening before they're ready for regression. Others will dive right into a past event, even in the first session. All you need to do is go with the flow.

I hope you can appreciate how this approach can help you and your client feel more confident moving forward with the Therapeutic Relationship. The client can relax about their first session because now they know what to expect. They know that the first session is going to prepare them for the work you will do together. And they don't have to decide anything further until after they've experienced that first session. As a result, they can relax.

You can relax, too, because the only thing you care about in the first session is making sure that you have a client who is ready for regression. That's much easier than trying to nail it in a single session, wouldn't you agree?

To be fair, the client won't really know what they're getting themselves into until they've been there. Even if they've been to a hypnotist before, your approach can be very different. A baby-step approach just makes it safer. This can make it easier for you to locate and resolve the causal event because safety is the Subconscious Mind's primary concern. Working with the Subconscious Mind will earn you powerful rapport with the part of the client that has the power to create real and lasting change.

Summary

Some clients will be apprehensive about the first session. This can result in no-shows. You can do away with no-shows by telling the client what will happen in the first session. What's going to happen? Talk. Teach. Relax.

The first session allows you to assess the client's readiness for regression. This can make your job easier by allowing you to prepare the client for the work you will do together.

The only thing the client needs to commit to is the first session. Once they have experienced working with you, they can decide how they wish to proceed with you.

Getting rid of the unrealistic expectation that you're going to fix a lifetime problem in a single session takes the pressure off both you and the client. This can help you to feel more confident moving forward with the Therapeutic Relationship.

A baby-step approach makes it safer for the client to take the next logical step. It makes it safer for you, too, by allowing you to assess the client's readiness for regression.

Following the first session, the client will better understand what they're signing up for. And you'll have a better idea of where to begin the healing process for that client.

CHAPTER 3:
The First Session

T he client's first session generally involves three steps—the intake process, the educational pre-talk, and the client's first hypnosis session. This can vary from client to client, but each step is essential for effective Regression Hypnotherapy.[6] No matter what happens, the client's first session with you should be a valuable learning experience.

Just talking about themselves and sharing their history without being judged can be a deeply healing experience for many clients. And once they have experienced their first hypnosis session with you, the client will have a better idea of what they're signing up for. They'll know that nothing bad will happen; that it's safe to let you guide them through the process. They may discover things about themselves that they hadn't realized or gain some insight into the nature of the problem. They may even experience a measure of relief. As a result, they'll be able to make a more informed decision to continue working with you. Success really is in your setup.

---

[6] You can learn the seven steps to effective Regression-to-Cause hypnotherapy in *The Devil's Therapy: Hypnosis Practitioner's Essential Guide to Effective Regression Hypnotherapy*.

The information you need to customize your educational pre-talk to meet each client's specific needs comes out of the intake process. This is why the intake process comes first. It tells you where to begin the healing work and how to make your educational pre-talk relevant to the client's needs and concerns. The intake gives you the information you need to guide the healing process effectively. This makes your intake an integral part of the healing process. As such, it needs to be an interactive process and not merely an exercise in filling out forms. This is also true of the educational pre-talk.

The Contract

The purpose of the educational pre-talk is to establish a Contract that makes the client a partner in their own healing. This Contract establishes who is responsible for what in order to achieve the client's Therapeutic Goal. However, the educational pre-talk for Regression Hypnotherapy needs to be more comprehensive than your basic hypnosis pre-talk because it requires two agreements:

1. Agreement to allow hypnosis
2. Agreement to allow regression

First, you need to establish a Contract that allows hypnosis to happen. Then, you need to establish a Contract that gives you permission to guide the client into events from the past. The process of establishing these Contracts begins with educating your client about how the Mind works.

While most people believe that they have a Mind, few give a moment's thought to how it actually works. When a person is thinking, feeling, or acting in ways they don't like, it's because their Conscious Mind and Subconscious Mind are not in alignment. There's an internal conflict.

But most people don't realize this. They just think that there's something wrong with them. They think they lack willpower or that they're defective and need fixing. Your educational pre-talk should show them why there's nothing wrong with them and why they don't need to be fixed. It's just how the Mind works.

The Mind is a wonderful thing. Everyone should have one. ~ **Ashleigh Brilliant**

Keep It Simple

Your Mind Model gives you a visual aid to show your client how hypnosis gives access to the cause of the problem. Pictures and images speak directly to the Subconscious Mind. This can help get rid of many unknowns, making it safe for the client to follow your instructions while proving that you can be trusted to guide them.

I have studied a variety of Mind Models, but, in the end, I found Freud's iceberg model to be most effective because it's simple. It clearly illustrates the distinction between the two levels of Mind— Conscious and Subconscious. Most clients quickly grasp how these two parts function very differently from one another. For example,

> "Whatever's going on above the surface of consciousness is just what we're consciously aware of. That's the Conscious Mind. But it's just the tip of the iceberg. There's a deeper level of awareness below the surface.

> "These two parts of the Mind function very differently. The Conscious Mind thinks. The Subconscious Mind feels. The Conscious Mind uses thinking, reasoning, and analysis to make sense of things and come up with solutions to problems.

"While the Conscious Mind is very useful when it comes to making out a grocery list, balancing the checkbook, or figuring out an eating plan, when it comes to dealing with feelings, not so much. That's because the Conscious Mind doesn't do feelings. It just *thinks*. Feeling is the territory of the Subconscious Mind.

"Both these parts of you are valuable and serve an important function. And great things can be accomplished when the Conscious Mind and Subconscious Mind work together. Our goal, working together, is to put you back in control by bringing these two parts of you back into alignment."

You're going to be asking the client to step into the emotional part of their Mind. You're going to ask them to allow the uncomfortable feelings and emotions they've been trying to avoid bubbling up to conscious awareness. You're going to ask them to follow those feelings back into the painful past events that caused them. You're going to ask them to face the memories and emotions that have everything to do with the unwanted symptoms. To do that, you need the client's permission. To gain their permission, you need to make what you're going to ask of them reasonable. Reason and logic speak to the Conscious Mind. For example,

"Some people say that the Conscious Mind only makes up about 5 percent of our mental potential. The other 95 percent is below the surface at the Subconscious level of mind. But no one really knows what the percentage really is. The Conscious Mind might be only 2 percent or 0.0001 percent. Who can say? Nobody has ever been able to measure the power of the Mind. But I heard it estimated that Einstein was using about 10 percent of his mental potential. He was considered a genius!

"Many of the 'big brains' like Albert Einstein, Thomas Edison, and Walt Disney took catnaps while working on a problem. They discovered that briefly setting aside 10 percent of their mental potential created space for the 90 percent to work on the problem. Essentially, that's what we do with hypnosis. Hypnosis temporarily sets aside the 5 percent so that you can gain access to the other 95 percent of your power.

"Research shows that, when we sleep, the Conscious Mind steps aside, creating space for the Subconscious Mind to go to work. Hypnosis isn't sleep. It's a setting-aside of the Conscious Mind to allow the Subconscious Mind to step forward. But many of the benefits of taking a catnap such as improved memory function, lower blood pressure, and reducing stress are also wonderful side-benefits of hypnosis."

The iceberg shows the client where the Power is. It's right there below the threshold of consciousness. They can clearly see that they *have* the Power they need to create the change they want. They just haven't been able to access it. That's why they need you! You can help them gain access to the other 95 percent of their Mental Potential. Make sure you point this out to the client; they haven't been successful because they've been relying on only 5 percent of their mental potential. That's not enough power to create the kind of change they want.

Show That It's Possible

Anchor your educational pre-talk to the client's issue. Establish that there's a difference between the Conscious Mind and the Subconscious Mind in terms of Power. Show how these two levels of Mind function very differently. Then, bring it back to the client's presenting issue and show why the change they desire is possible. That's why they're seeing you. For example,

> "While the Conscious Mind is very smart and capable, the Subconscious Mind's job is to hold onto all our memories of past experiences and how they made us feel. That's because the Subconscious Mind's primary concern is with our survival. It's always there to protect us and support us in being successful in life *based on what we learned* from our history. What makes anything memorable is how it makes us feel. What we learned from past experiences was meant to make us smarter and better able to meet our own needs.

> "At the deepest level, there's a Part of us that never changes. Some people call this the Unconscious Mind. This Part of you holds onto your genetic blueprint for well-being. Think of it as your core programming for health and happiness. It's what tells us how to feel good and be happy and loving towards ourselves and others.

> "It's human nature to seek to be happy. It's in our design. The goal of the healing process is to reconnect with this Part of you because that's the *real* Power. It's in you now. You were created to be happy, whole, and complete. That means that, at your Core, you are, and you remain, exactly as you were designed.

> "It's just that stuff happened, growing up, that caused us to lose touch with ourselves. It happens to everyone. We forget who we are and how to feel good about ourselves.

"When we reconnect with this internal blueprint for health and happiness, healing happens. That's when we feel most ourselves. We feel happy and in harmony with ourselves and with Life. We feel good.

"The good news is . . . you haven't changed. The blueprint is still there, along with all your good feelings."

Make It Relevant

The key to an effective pre-talk is customizing it to be relevant to the client's specific circumstances, presenting problem, and personal history. For example, if you're speaking to a client with anxiety, you could talk about how experiences in life taught us to fear and how what has been learned can be un-learned. You could talk about how their ability to feel safe and confident, and experience trust in the world, is still there inside them. The goal of the healing process would then be to reconnect with those abilities.

The habits we form from childhood make no small difference, but rather they make all the difference.

~ Aristotle

Physical Symptoms

If it was a person with a physical ailment, you could talk about the healing power of the Mind. You could talk about how there's a healing intelligence in every cell of the body and how the body already knows how to heal. This is obvious to anyone. If you cut a finger, it heals. If you get a bruise, it heals. You could talk about how it's in our nature to heal. It's right there in our blueprint for health and well-being. We're all born with it. We never lose it, which means that it's still there. It's just that something is blocking it. We can change that.

Behavioral Symptoms

If you're speaking to a person with a habit problem, you could talk about it as a learned behavior that was initially meant to be helpful. Make the Subconscious Mind friendly. It's not the enemy. It's there to take care of us. It's just that, sometimes, it needs a little help. For example,

> "The ability to do things automatically, or habitually, frees up the Conscious Mind to focus on other things. That's good because the Conscious Mind is limited. It doesn't have the power to run everything. Fortunately, once you've learned how to do something like walking, tying your shoelaces, riding a bicycle, or driving a car, the Subconscious Mind can make the behavior automatic. When that happens, it becomes a habit.

> "A habit means you don't have to think about it anymore. It means that you can multi-task. You can get more done. This makes you awesomely efficient. Being efficient serves survival, which just happens to be your Subconscious Mind's Prime Directive. It's there to keep you safe.

> "You can be driving the car while your mind wanders off. You can be thinking about where you've been or where you're going. And while you're lost in thought, who do you think is driving the car? When your Conscious Mind wanders off into Lah-Lah Land, your Subconscious Mind takes over. It makes sure that you get home safely because it's there to protect you. Here's where things get interesting. The same is true of reaching for a cigarette . . . or grabbing a candy bar when we feel stressed or tired.

"The Subconscious Mind *must* protect you. That's its primary concern. If doing that satisfied a need in the past—it works. If reaching for a cigarette or grabbing a candy bar helped you feel better or cope, Subconsciously, that helped you survive. As a result, the Subconscious Mind will make sure that you continue to do that because it's meeting an important need.

"The problem is that, when that happens, the Conscious Mind is going to struggle to change the behavior. The Conscious Mind just doesn't have the power to override a Subconscious survival strategy. And because the Subconscious Mind doesn't think, it doesn't discriminate between a 'good' behavior and a 'bad' behavior. All the Subconscious Mind knows is that if it helped in the past, *it works*, so it's going to store that pattern in memory for future reference.

"That's what's there at the Subconscious level of Mind—feelings and memories from the past. Memories are a record of what we learned from experience. Learning serves survival. Based on those learnings, we formed beliefs. Our beliefs then decide how we think, feel, and act in daily life. It's all based on what we learned in the past. Some people call this programming.

"Bruce Lipton, the author of *The Biology of Belief*, says that most of our programming got established before the age of five or six. Most people are shocked to hear this because this means that many of the beliefs that are running our adult lives got started long before we could reason!

"What we find in Regression sessions is that many problems get started very early in life, often before the age of two. That's long before a person can think for themselves. It's also why sometimes it can feel like a two-year-old is running your life!

"Think about how much you had to learn during the first two years of life. You learned to walk, talk, feed yourself, dress, and tie your shoelaces. All the intricacies of a language involve a tremendous amount of learning. Adults struggle to learn a second language. But a child can quickly grasp multiple languages if taught early enough in life.

"Some experts suggest that more learning occurs in the first two years than will happen over the course of a person's remaining lifetime. Pretty impressive, when you think about it, isn't it? But this much we know: Many of the beliefs that are running *your* life tell you what to expect from life, formed before you were old enough to think for yourself.

"Our beliefs tell us how the world works. They tell us how to get our needs met. They tell us how to be, and not be, in order to get love and approval, or how to avoid the pain of disapproval and punishment. We learned how relationships work by what was modeled to us by others. The things that were said or done to us taught us what to expect from others. From this, we decided what we deserved.

"Our Core Beliefs are based on the perceptions of a Child. And some of the beliefs, or automatic responses, that we developed in childhood are simply no longer relevant to us as adults. But the Subconscious Mind doesn't know this because the Subconscious Mind doesn't think. It just runs things automatically and doesn't forget a thing because this ability to learn from experience has helped us survive and evolve as a species.

"This doesn't mean that a memory is necessarily based in truth or fact, however. It's simply a recording of perceptions, thoughts, and feelings associated with a specific set of circumstances. It's just how we interpreted those things at that time. Memory is a recording of what we learned, based on the knowledge and understanding we had, at the age those things happened. Those experiences formed the basis of our beliefs.

"This is where we can have a problem—our beliefs decide what we're going to get in life. But they're not necessarily based on fact. All we can say for certain is that stuff happened. Decisions were made. We did our best to make sense of things. But mistakes were made. Most of the time, the problem is just an error in perception. Children routinely misperceive things around them. That's forgivable—which means it can be changed. Anything that's been learned can be unlearned simply by accessing the part of the Mind that holds onto feelings and memories. But to communicate with that part of the Mind, we need to use a different language than the Conscious Mind.

"The Conscious Mind uses reason and logic. The Subconscious Mind uses images and emotions. This is the same language as dreams. We can have daydreams and night dreams. We can picture things, and we can recall memories. We want to pay attention during hypnosis because this is how the Subconscious Mind communicates.

"The Subconscious Mind also speaks through sensations in the body because the Subconscious Mind is the Feeling Mind. We feel our feelings in the body. They might be sensations of tightness, or pressure, or emotions like fear, anger, or sadness.

"When you're in hypnosis, you're more aware of these things. We want to give attention to feelings and emotions because that's the Subconscious Mind speaking. And the Subconscious Mind knows how the problem got started.

"It also has the power to change things. It just needs a little help. This is where hypnosis can help. Hypnosis is what gives us access to the Subconscious Mind."

When you educate a client about how the Mind works, make it all about the client. Don't make it about the hypnosis. Make it relevant to the client's problem and personal history so they'll pay attention. Remember, they don't care about the hypnosis. The only thing they care about is—how will this help me get rid of the problem? Speak to that.

Hypnosis requires focused attention. Making your educational pre-talk visual and relevant to the client's problem will hold their attention. When you offer reasons and logic, you're speaking directly to the Conscious Mind. When you use a visual model to illustrate how the Mind works, you speak directly to the Subconscious Mind. You're delivering suggestions in a way that satisfies both the Conscious and Subconscious minds.

Summary

Before you can teach the client how to participate in their healing, you first need to establish that they have a Conscious Mind and a

Subconscious Mind. Your Mind Model comes first in your educational pre-talk because it shows the client *why* they haven't resolved the problem and how hypnosis can help.

The Conscious Mind needs to understand because understanding gives a sense of control. Satisfy that need, and you'll have the client's undivided attention. Use numbers, percentages, comparisons, reason, and logic. Show the client how the Conscious Mind doesn't have the power. The power is at a deeper level of Mind. Hypnosis gives us access to the Part of them that's holding onto 95 percent of their mental potential. This makes hypnosis reasonable. Satisfy their Conscious Mind's need for reason, and your clients will be much more cooperative when it comes time to do the hypnosis.

Use the language of the Subconscious Mind by using pictures to illustrate how the Mind works. Show that it's okay for the client to go where you will lead them, and you will satisfy the Subconscious Mind's need for safety. Show the client that there's nothing wrong with them; it's just how the Mind's designed.

Show them that they have the power to create the change they want; it's right there beneath the surface. Help the client to realize that they're in the right place. You're going to help them to gain access to that power. Not only does this empower the client by providing a sense of hope, but it also sets you up to establish the Contract for hypnosis.

Conscious Mind	Subconscious Mind
Thinking Mind • The leading edge of thought • Limited • Compares and contrasts • Selective Attention • Makes Decisions	**Feeling Mind** • The Conscious Mind of the Past • Unlimited • Sorts and stores • Direct Download • Cannot make decisions
Limited • 10% of our Mental Potential • Must prioritize, i.e., what is relevant • Is limited to 7 to 9 bits of information (+/- 2) or 40 nerve impulses per second • Needs to sleep • Forgets • Relies on willpower to control • Thinks it's running the show	**Unlimited** • 90% of our Mental Potential • Has unlimited capacity for learning • Can process 40 million nerve impulses per second • Never sleeps; runs 24/7, 365 in the background • Never forgets • Where the Real Power is at • Is running the show
Compares and contrasts • Gathers and processes relevant information from environment • Analyzes and evaluates to make meaning • Makes decisions based on meaning • Constructs a Story to make sense of experiences • Uses linear timeline	**Sorts and stores** • Forms connections; links aspects of experience together • Stores experience as memory • Generalizes all learning; reinforces what is already known, i.e., "safe" • Compounds familiar patterns • Totally in the Now

Selective Attention (Conscious)	Direct Download (Unconscious)
• Is only aware of what you are paying attention to at the moment • Language of reason and rationale • Forms beliefs and expectations	• Accepts impressions from environment • Doesn't discriminate (doesn't think) • Language of Image and Emotion • Holds onto beliefs and expectations
Makes Decisions based on Story • True/False • Good/Bad • Right/Wrong • Safe/Unsafe	**Cannot Decide because it doesn't think** • Cannot distinguish truth from untruth • Runs programs based on learning • Performs functions automatically, i.e., habits
Creative • Uses thinking to override feelings • Re-members by re-assembling pieces of information stored in memory • Re-constructs information into interesting new ideas or meaning • Prime Directive is to achieve rewards • Wants control	**Protective** • Drives behaviors and responses • Communicates with Conscious Mind • Uses symbolic language based on past experiences (implicit and explicit) • Prime Directive is to protect • Wants to survive/thrive

Health is a state of complete physical, mental and social well-being and not merely the absence of disease or infirmity.

~ World Health Organization

CHAPTER 4:
Contract for Hypnosis

P eople don't pay for hypnosis. They pay for results. Hypnosis is just a tool you use to help them to achieve their desired results. But most people don't know this because most people don't know much about hypnosis. What they do know is often contaminated by myths, misconceptions, and erroneous beliefs. You need to correct erroneous assumptions before guiding the client into hypnosis.

*Hypnosis is a state of mind in which the critical faculty of the human is bypassed, and selective thinking established. ~ **Dave Elman***

There are lots of definitions of hypnosis. But even hypnosis professionals can't agree on what it is. Technically, hypnosis has to do with by-passing the Critical Faculty of the Mind. But that's too fancy pants for most clients. For the purposes of educating a client in readiness for Regression Hypnotherapy, it's best to keep things simple. All the client really needs to know is that hypnosis is focused concentration. This tells them what to do. For example,

"Hypnosis is a state of focused attention where you set aside thinking and analyzing. When the Thinking Part of the Mind takes a back seat, the Feeling Part of Mind is allowed to step forward so that we can interact with it."

Hypnosis Happens

The client thinks they're paying you for the hypnosis. What they're really paying for are the results. But to get those results, the client needs to know that they were hypnotized. Before you start guiding them into past events, you need to satisfy this need. If you don't, they'll be preoccupied with thinking, "Am I hypnotized?" Or, "Is it happening?" That will only be in the way.

The place to begin is by educating the client about what they can expect to experience when hypnosis happens. For example,

"Hypnosis is a natural, normal state. Everybody experiences hypnosis. But it's different for everyone. It's a highly individual experience.

"People naturally go in and out of hypnosis throughout the day. It's a natural process we all experience. It's called the Basic Rest Activity Cycle (BRAC). The BRAC is the body-mind's natural healing cycle.

"The body-mind system needs frequent breaks throughout the day. As a result, every 90—120 minutes, whether you're aware of it or not, your Conscious Mind activity gets set aside temporarily. It takes a little break for about twenty minutes.

"During this rest period, the body-mind system gets a much-needed break. When you emerge, you feel refreshed. It's like a system re-boot.

"Most people don't even realize when it's happening. It just happens automatically. For example, if your Mind has ever wandered off while you're driving the car, and you took the wrong turn, or missed the exit on the freeway, you know what I'm talking about. Your Conscious Mind took a break, and your Subconscious Mind took over.

"Your Subconscious Mind stepped forward to take care of you. That's its job—to keep you safe. We have all experienced this. That's why there's a name for it. It's called "Highway Hypnosis." Some people call it "Road Trance." It happens all the time—watching TV, reading a book, losing time when you're engaged in a hobby."

You need the client to be willing to set aside thinking and analyzing. If they're trying to figure out whether or not the hypnosis is happening, that will prevent it from happening. That won't help you to get the results you want. You can encourage this conscious compliance before you begin the induction. For example,

"Have you ever sat in the classroom and had your mind wander off? The next thing you know, you 'come to' and realize that you've missed the last twenty minutes of the lecture? You weren't asleep. What happened is that the Conscious Mind took a seat on the sidelines allowing your Subconscious Mind to take over. That's hypnosis. Hypnosis happens. It's a very natural experience."

Hypnosis is Not Sleep

A lot of people think that hypnosis is sleep. As a result, they think they're going to lie back and have a snooze while you do all the work. That's not very helpful. To pre-empt this, I like to borrow a phrase from C. Roy Hunter. "If you go to sleep, it will be the most expensive nap you've ever taken!" That usually gets a chuckle from the client, and it corrects the misperception that they're going to be asleep or that napping is, in any way, desirable. It's not.

Hypnosis is Not Relaxation

Many people think that hypnosis is relaxation. While Relaxation Hypnosis is the easiest way to begin the healing process for most clients, it is not appropriate for every client. You need to match the induction to the client. The client needs to understand that hypnosis is not relaxation. It is a by-passing of the Critical Faculty of the Mind that gives access to the Subconscious level of Mind. You don't need relaxation for that.

Relaxation is often a wonderful side benefit of hypnosis. But hypnosis is *not* relaxation, and the client doesn't need to be able to relax to experience hypnosis. This is an important distinction to make for two reasons. First, some people have so much tension and anxiety that they can't relax. If they think they have to relax to experience hypnosis, they won't believe that they were hypnotized. If they don't believe that they were hypnotized, they won't believe change can happen. The change they want depends on their belief.

Second, Therapeutic Hypnosis is an interactive process that requires experiencing uncomfortable feelings. This means that, sometimes, the client won't feel relaxed. This doesn't mean that they're not in hypnosis. Far from it! To access a feeling, conscious awareness must cross the threshold between the Conscious and Subconscious levels of Mind.

The Subconscious Mind is the emotional Mind. This means that when a person is experiencing an emotion, they're in a state of hypnosis. The stronger the emotion, the deeper the hypnosis.

Teach your clients that hypnosis is not relaxation and that it does not require relaxation. Let them know that a person can be in a very deep state of hypnosis and not even realize it. Reassure them that they don't need to be able to relax to experience hypnosis. If the client knows what to expect, they'll feel safe in letting it happen. All that's required is that they set aside Conscious Mind activity, and hypnosis will happen very easily.

For the purposes of the first session, whenever possible, Relaxation Hypnosis can be very useful because it's a very gentle, pleasant experience. This ensures that the client's first experience with you will be a positive one. It's also the ideal state to teach the client how to work with you. For example,

> "During the first session, I'm going teach you how to relax into a nice, comfortable state of hypnosis. During this session, I will be giving you instructions to relax the body. Mind and body do not function independently. So, as you *follow my instructions* to allow the body to relax, the Mind will naturally follow, allowing you to enjoy a beautiful state of hypnosis."

Most people don't have any resistance to relaxing. This makes Relaxation Hypnosis the easiest way for a person to learn how to enter a state of hypnosis. All they have to do is follow your instructions, and you'll get them there. You can then use the sensations of deepening relaxation as evidence that hypnosis is happening. (Remember, that's what they *think* they're paying for!) For example,

> "Hypnosis happens when we let it. It's a very natural experience. There's nothing to do or try. Just let that wonderful Thinking Part of you take a little break. It can just sit off on the sidelines and be curious about the process. This will allow the hypnosis to happen very naturally. Okay?"[7]

Hypnosis Doesn't Feel Like Anything

Close your eyes and notice how you feel. That's what hypnosis feels like. If you're conducting a Relaxation Hypnosis session, you can associate the feelings of deepening relaxation to the hypnosis. But hypnosis doesn't feel like anything. The client needs to know this. Hypnosis is a state that you will guide them into. You will then test to verify that they're there. Let the client know that most people don't realize it when they're in hypnosis.

If the client has a need to know, you can share some of the more observable common signs of hypnosis which they may, or may not, be aware of during the session:

1. **Pink eye.** Relaxation in the eyeball allows greater blood flow. The blood vessels dilate, causing blood to rush into the white area of the eyeball.

2. **Rapid Eye Movement (REM).** The eyeballs move back and forth behind the eyelids indicating visual activity is occurring.

---

[7] When you ask "Okay?" and the client agrees, you have established a Contract. In this case, the client is agreeing to set aside conscious mental activity. Reinforce this agreement throughout your pre-talk.

3. **Eye Roll** (occurs in deeply relaxed states). The eyes roll up and back in the sockets leaving only the whites showing.

4. **Lacrimation or teary eyes.** It occurs when the tear-ducts relax to the point of watering involuntarily.

5. **Salivation.** Salivary glands may increase the production of saliva in the mouth resulting in increased swallowing.

6. **Eyelid flutter.** As the muscles in the eyelid relax, the nerves jump.

7. **Muscle fasciculation.** Twitching or jerks in the small muscles occur as the nervous system releases tension.

8. **Change in body temperature.** Changes in body temperature are due to pulse rate and circulation of blood. Warmth is the more common subjective experience. The client may also notice tingling sensations as blood flow increases.

9. **Change in breathing.** Breathing may be faster or slower. Deep sighs occur when the brain requires more oxygen to deal with a new or fearful situation or when releasing stress.

10. **Face flushes**. Increased circulation may result in blotchiness in the face and neck. (More common with men.)

11. **Lethargic, limp state.** This is triggered by the release of chemical relaxants from the brain (endorphins). During a Relaxation Hypnosis session, the client may experience sensations of sinking or floating.

Hypnosis is Not Stage Hypnotism

Clients can have fears about the hypnosis that they won't mention to you. Then, when it comes time to do the hypnosis, you can find yourself bumping into resistance. It's not that the client is being difficult. It's just that you haven't addressed some worry or concern, and they're feeling afraid. That's what resistance is—fear. Usually, the problem is that they have seen a stage hypnosis show or a Hollywood movie, and they think. "That's hypnosis." As a result, they think that you can control them. You can resolve this misconception during your pre-talk by mentioning stage hypnotism. Most of the time, the client won't bother to ask you about it. But if you bring it up, they'll say, "Yah, I was wondering about that . . ."

You can then teach them how what you do is different from stage hypnotism. What the client needs to understand is that stage hypnotists are entertainers. They use hypnosis for entertainment. For example,

> "Stage hypnosis is great fun. That's its purpose—to entertain. These days many stage hypnotists are also highly skilled therapists. But stage hypnotism is 'show biz'" *Therapeutic* Hypnosis is for healing. I have seen some amazing stage hypnosis shows. But this is different. *Therapeutic* Hypnosis is for healing, not entertainment."

If the client thinks they're going to be Svengali-ed,[8] they won't believe they were hypnotized. Make sure that they understand that hypnosis is not something *you* do. It's something that *they* will do by following your instructions. For example,

> "For stage hypnosis, you need volunteers. A person has to want it and be willing to follow instructions. For this reason, the best stage shows are BIG because there will be more people to select from the audience to be a part of the show. Let's face

[8] Svengali is a character in a novel who used hypnosis to manipulate and control a young Irish girl and make her into a famous singer.

it—not everyone is going to be willing to get up on stage in front of everyone and cluck like a chicken. This is why the best audiences are college kids. College kids will do anything! They're curious and open to new experiences. They're willing to have fun. They really *are* the show.

"Healing hypnosis requires your participation. So, you're never asleep, you're never unconscious. In fact, when you're in hypnosis, you're much more aware. During the session, you'll have full awareness so that you can participate. That's what we want. If you have full awareness, you'll have full control.

"Most people don't realize this, but hypnosis is a hyper-alert state. You're much more aware than you are normally. The deeper you go into hypnosis, the deeper you go into the Subconscious Mind, and the more aware you become of thoughts, feelings, memories, and emotions. That's good.

"All hypnosis is, really, a shift of focus. Instead of thinking and analyzing, you're paying attention to feelings. The more you allow feelings (sensations and emotions) to come to awareness, the more access you have to the Subconscious Mind. That's where your answers lie."

Establish a Contract

Healing is about restoring a person's ability to feel good—physically, mentally, and emotionally. To achieve that goal, you need your client to be an active participant in the process. This is because they have the ability to block the healing. This begins by making your educational pre-talk an interactive process. Make it more of a conversation than a presentation. Invite questions. Offer clarification.

Encouraging better understanding gives the Conscious Mind what it wants—a sense of control. This makes it safe for the thinking part of the Mind to take a backseat, allowing you to guide the client into hypnosis. Remember, the client can override the healing process by engaging in thinking. They can block the healing from happening by putting a lid on their feelings.

Begin by reminding the client that thinking won't get them the result they're after. For example,

> "Remember, thinking, analyzing, or trying to figure things out is using the wrong part of the Mind. It's trying to use 5 percent of the Power to move 95 percent of the problem. Clearly, this isn't a good strategy. That's why there's a problem, to begin with. But you already know this. You've already tried thinking your way out of the problem. There really is a better way. For example,

> "The way out of the problem is to access the Part of the Mind that has the Power you need to heal yourself. You just need to be willing to set aside thinking and reasoning and pay attention to the feelings instead. If you think about it, this makes sense. Thinking speeds up brain activity. Healing requires exactly the opposite—slowing down."

To be successful, you need compliance. Compliance means cooperation. You need the client's cooperation to be successful because you can't do it for them. The client must agree to set aside the need for control and let thinking take a back seat. Without that agreement, the Conscious Mind will just get in your way.

If you make it safe for the client to "go there" before you start asking them to go there, you'll have much less resistance to deal with when it comes time to do the hypnosis. For example,

> "We want that mental activity associated with the Adult, Thinking Part of the Mind to be set aside. At least to begin with. The Adult, Thinking Part of you is an essential part of the healing process, too. When the time comes, I will be calling upon it to assist in the process. But until then, I need the Conscious Mind to be willing to take a back seat. Just let that Thinking Part of you sit off on the sidelines until I call upon it. Until then, that Part of you takes on the role of observer, understand?"

Invite the client to set aside fear and be curious instead. An inquisitive state of mind opens the client to learning and discovery. Not only does this help to reduce unnecessary resistance, but it also gives you a more resourceful client to work with. For example,

> "You can be curious about what might happen and what you might learn. Healing is, after all, a process of self-discovery and self-empowerment. It's okay to suspend judgment temporarily. If you want to, you can think about it later. Later it will all make sense. You'll be much wiser for it, after the fact. Okay?"

Summary

Hypnosis is not what most people think. What they do know is often contaminated by myths, misconceptions, and erroneous beliefs. You need to uncover and correct these erroneous assumptions before guiding the client into hypnosis. Make it safe for the client to follow your instructions to enter into a state of hypnosis by teaching them that hypnosis is no big deal. It's natural. Everybody does it. They've already done it a thousand times. Hypnosis happens very easily when we let it!

Hypnosis is not sleep or unconsciousness. The client will have full awareness, which means they'll have full control. This makes it safe.

Hypnosis is not relaxation. Nor does it require relaxation. However, Relaxation Hypnosis is the easiest way to learn how to enter into a state of hypnosis and enjoy it. Using relaxation in the first session allows you to prove that hypnosis happened by anchoring the feelings and sensations of relaxation to the state of hypnosis.

Stage hypnotism is for entertainment. Therapeutic Hypnosis is for healing. In both cases, a person has to want to go into the state of hypnosis.

Regression Hypnotherapy requires the client's participation. For this reason, your pre-talk should be an interactive process. Make it more of a conversation than a presentation.

The Contract for hypnosis is an agreement to set aside conscious mental activity and shift attention onto feelings and emotions. The client must agree to let the Conscious Mind take a back seat.

Inviting a sense of curiosity can help to instill a more open-minded willingness to learn and discover. This is a more resourceful state and can help to reduce unnecessary resistance.

CHAPTER 5:
Symptoms of the Problem

ymptoms are the reason clients come to you for help. They might be struggling with a behavioral, physical, or emotional problem, but whatever the client thinks is the problem is seldom the whole problem. It's merely a symptom of an unresolved problem that exists at the Subconscious level of Mind. Regression Hypnotherapy is based on the idea that every problem is the result of a life experience. Symptoms don't simply arise out of nothing. Something happened to cause the problem.

Often, the client's problem has roots in a stressful experience in childhood. It's because the Subconscious Mind has been unable to find a solution to the real problem that it generates symptoms. The purpose of symptoms is to make the unconscious conscious. This Subconscious requirement for symptoms is called the Symptom Imperative (SI). Regression Hypnotherapy focuses on finding the source of the Symptom Imperative by locating the Initial Sensitizing Event (ISE).

Every problem you'll deal with in your sessions has roots in some kind of stressful experience in the past. The fundamental problem is that the Subconscious Mind is timeless. It doesn't recognize that situations, which caused the client pain in the past, are over. As a result, the client is hyper-sensitive to situations in daily life that act as reminders of the unresolve ISE. These Subsequent Sensitizing Events (SSE) trigger events that re-stimulate the underlying, unresolved pain pattern, adding to the accumulated internal stress. Eventually, the problem finds expression through symptoms. That's when the client realizes, "Houston, we have a problem!"

"The lump, the bump, the ache, the pain—physical or emotional—is just how the Subconscious Mind makes an important need known to the Conscious Mind. The symptom is a signal. It's coming out of the Subconscious Mind and, like a compass, points to the source of the problem."

~ **The Devil's Therapy**

The Stress Factor

Everybody's got stress. One estimate is that 97 percent of all conditions being treated by primary healthcare workers is stress related. Stress affects both cognition and biology. It suppresses the immune response, inhibits brain function, makes muscle and joint pain worse. Stress can also trigger emotional problems which affect the body. Dr. Alex Lloyd, the author of *The Healing Codes*,[9] states that stress is THE underlying

---

[9] This book is a great resource because most of the issues that clients will come to you for help with are caused by or exacerbated by stress. You'll find lots of information you can use for educating clients about the effects of everyday stress.

cause of every problem. While stress affects each of us differently, there's little doubt that many of the problems that clients come to you for help with are either caused by or made worse by stress. As most people can relate to feeling stressed, teaching your client about the stress-response can help them to make the connection between how their Mind and body work together. For example,

> "Stress is defined as the body's natural response to any perceived threat, real or imagined. Whenever we perceive a threat, it sets off a cascade of responses in the body that generate symptoms of discomfort. That's the body's stress response.

> "Human beings are hard-wired for survival. The problem is that our biology hasn't changed much since the days of our Paleolithic cousins. Unlike us, they had real dangers to deal with in their environment. Imagine stepping out your front door and facing a saber-toothed tiger! At that moment, the last thing you need to do is to think! Thinking will only slow you down. For the cave man, it was survival of the quickest. The slower you were, the better your chances were of becoming somebody's lunch.

> "The stress-response gives us the ability to respond automatically, without thought. This is what helped us to survive as a species. It's because, during the stress response, thinking shuts down while the body prepares us to take action to ensure our safety. That's good. The problem is that the body

---

You can also use this information to create presentations for educating the public about what you do.

can't think. It feels. In the face of a threat, you don't need to think. You need to move. You need to run away or defend yourself NOW—not think about it for a while and devise a strategy.

"The Subconscious Mind's Prime Directive is to protect us. To fulfill its mission, the Subconscious Mind holds onto our feelings and memories. That's its job. This ensures that we'll know how to respond to similar situations in the future.

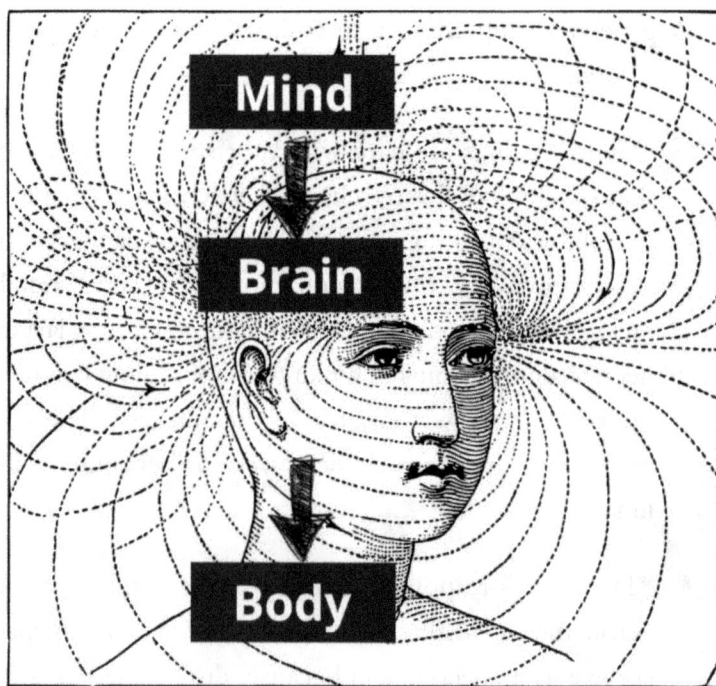

"The Mind perceives what's happening through our five-sensory channels of perception. We see, hear, smell, taste and feel what's happening in our environment. These perceptions make an impression on the brain. The brain then conceives a signal based on the nature of the perception.

"If what's happening is perceived as safe, the brain will generate the all-clear. If there's a perceived threat, it will sound the alarm. This signal takes the form of stress hormones like cortisol, adrenalin, and norepinephrine. These hormones put the body on red alert. They also don't feel good because the body is responding to a threat. Stress hormones tell the body to get ready to take action and ensure your survival by either fighting or fleeing.

"That's the Subconscious Mind's Prime Directive—survival. But there's a problem. The Subconscious Mind doesn't know the difference between a real and a psychological threat. It simply responds to the signal. If something is perceived as a threat, the body will automatically respond *as if* the situation was life-threatening. If you've ever been startled by a snake, only to realize it was just the garden hose, or awakened from a nightmare with your heart pounding and the bedsheets kicked off, you know what I'm talking about. That's your Subconscious Mind at work, fulfilling its Prime Directive.

"Obviously, this ability to respond automatically, without thought, is a good thing—if you happen to live in a place where saber-toothed tigers are a problem. But for most of us, that's just not the case. We don't have to deal with lions, and tigers, and bears (oh-my!) on a daily basis. What we have are imagined threats.

"We have time pressures and too much to do. We have too much information and not enough time. We have arguments with spouses, and kids, and bosses.

"We have health worries, and money worries, and frustration dealing with bureaucracy. What this gets us is *chronic* stress. Stress is the Subconscious Mind responding to a perceived threat and putting us into a fight-or-flight. Chronic stress is what happens when the alarm switch stays ON. It keeps the body on red alert. This means the body is constantly being flooded with stress hormones like cortisol and adrenalin, and norepinephrine.

"These hormones disrupt every system in the body, and they generate dis-ease. For example, excess cortisol kills brain cells. This can generate mental fogginess, forgetfulness, and confusion. Cortisol affects metabolism, regulating blood sugar. It can generate carb cravings and weight gain. Norepinephrine raises blood pressure. It's a contributing factor to hypertension and is believed to play a role in ADHD and depression."

Diagnosis

A client who is dealing with a physical condition has often been given a diagnosis. A diagnosis is a label that allows a physician to prescribe a treatment. While a diagnosis can give the client some measure of relief—at least now they know what they're dealing with—the label makes the symptom more real. Now, it has a name. Now, it has an identity. Now it's separate from the client, which means that the client is powerless to change it. It's outside of their control. As a result, they can end up feeling like a victim of the dis-ease.

This perception of dis-ease as an enemy separates the client from their body. That's a big problem because the client has psychologically cut themselves off from the part of them that knows how to heal. Interestingly, this is the "surgical" solution. When dis-ease is the enemy, the solution is to cut it out. The body then becomes a battlefield and, until the problem is resolved, the client is sleeping with the enemy. What the client needs to know is that the body is not the enemy. It knows how to heal. When it doesn't, there's always a reason.

Dis-ease is not the body running amok. Every dis-ease is the result of a life experience that generated a stress response in the body. The way to change a person's biology is by re-evaluating the thoughts, feelings, and perceptions that keep triggering the fight-or-flight response. But to do that, you need to help the client view their Subconscious Mind as friendly and helpful. For example,

> "The body cannot make decisions. It just does what it's told. Only the Mind can make decisions. A decision is a thought. Thoughts generate emotions. Emotions drive human behavior.

> "Essentially, this is what Regression Hypnosis is about. It's about locating the initial perception—real or imagined—that's responsible for the whole unwanted pattern. You'll find that this pattern of thoughts, feelings, reactions/behavior has roots in unresolved stress from the past.

> "The Conscious Mind hasn't been able to think a way out of the problem because it doesn't know what the real problem is. It doesn't have all the information. The Subconscious Mind has the information, but it doesn't know how to fix the problem. We can change that because our Subconscious Mind knows what the *real* problem is. Let's ask it!"

The client needs to know that stress isn't all bad. Stressors in childhood are nature's way of helping us to develop resilience by teaching us how to respond. Surviving threat situations makes us stronger, faster, smarter, and more capable of surviving. New research shows that the harmful effects of stressful experiences are not inevitable. We believe that stress is bad. That's a problem because it generates internal resistance.

It's the internal resistance to the uncomfortable feelings that's destructive. When a person views their stress-response as helpful, there's no resistance. As a result, instead of dis-ease, they create the biology of courage and resilience. It seems that Friedrich Nietzsche was right. What doesn't kill us really does make us stronger!

As a hypnosis practitioner, you can help your clients transform how they perceive themselves and the world around them. You can help them revisit stressful situations in the past that had them running for cover. You can help them re-evaluate those situations using Adult Wisdom. In this way, you can transform a person's biology from one of stress and dis-ease to one of health and peace.

Summary

Stress is how the body automatically responds to any perceived threat. Stress hormones feel uncomfortable because the body is getting ready to take action in order to keep you safe. The problem is that the Subconscious Mind cannot discriminate between a real and an imagined threat. If something is perceived as a threat, the Subconscious Mind will automatically generate a response that is congruent with the nature of the perception.

Stress affects both cognition and biology. It makes physical and emotional pain worse. Virtually every issue clients come to you for help with is either caused by or exacerbated by stress.

Chronic stress happens when the alarm switch stays ON, keeping the body on red alert and flooded with stress hormones. These hormones disrupt every system in the body and generate dis-ease.

Dis-ease is not the body running amok because the body cannot make decisions. It can only do what it's told. The Mind perceives. The brain conceives. The body achieves.

A medical diagnosis can bring a sense of relief by validating that there is a problem. The label, however, creates a separation in the Mind of the client, making the body the enemy. This creates an internal conflict which leaves the client feeling powerless to an external force.

Every dis-ease has roots in a stressful life experience. The way to change a person's biology is by re-evaluating the perceptions, thoughts, and feelings associated with the stress response in the event that caused it.

The harmful effects of stress are not inevitable. Stressors in childhood are nature's way of making us stronger and more able to survive. Painful experiences were meant to teach us how to respond to life experiences. When a person views a painful past event through this lens, they create the biology of courage and resistance.

The way to transform a person's biology from one of dis-ease to one of health and peace is to revisit and re-evaluate the stressful situations in the past that generated the stress response.

Solve a problem by digging up its cause. Then the problem will no longer have a basis on which to stand. ~ **Christine DeLorey**

CHAPTER 6:
The Real Problem

The problems that people experience in adult life often have their roots in childhood. This is because children lack the maturity and resources needed to be able to cope with stressful situations. When a child feels overwhelmed or cannot find the solution to a problem, it needs help. When help doesn't come, the child can get emotionally stuck in that experience.

Stressful experiences early in life often turn out to be no big deal, at least to adult consciousness. But when a child cannot find a way out of a problem, it forms a Part of the personality. Parts, which formed in childhood, are Feeling Parts, more commonly referred to as Inner Child Parts. We have many, many Inner Child Parts—Happy Parts, Scared Parts, Curious Parts, Sad Parts. Many of the core Parts of the personality were shaped by specific experiences in early life.

A Problem of Time

To resolve the underlying cause of the problem, you will be inviting the client to consciously step into an event from the past and be a loving support to their Inner Child. To do this, the client needs to consciously recognize that there is a Part of them that is still stuck in a past event, trying to find a way out, and that this Part of them has been expressing through the symptoms because it needs help. The Part is not the problem. It's a problem of time. For example,

"The Conscious Mind is very linear. It's able to organize events in a way that helps us to make sense of our experiences. This provides us with a sense of control.

"Our language reflects this. We talk about putting the past behind us and looking ahead to the future. We can even picture neural pathways in the brain as little roads or railway tracks along which thoughts, feelings, and memories travel. But this linear model of time is really a construct of the Conscious Mind.

"The Subconscious Mind doesn't keep track of time the same way as the Conscious Mind. The Subconscious Mind is timeless. It's completely in the Now. Because of this, it has no problem with you being a five-month-old, a five-year-old, and a fifty-year-old, all simultaneously! Weird, I know. But it is this quality of the Subconscious Mind that makes regression possible. This is what allows your fifty-year-old self to go back into a past event and re-experience being a five-year-old. It's because, as far as your Subconscious Mind is concerned, it's all happening *still*. It doesn't realize that *that event is over*.

"The Subconscious Mind also has no problem with you being a Child *and* a Grownup at the same time. This is because, Subconsciously, there's no separation between you as a Child and your Grown-up self. They just exist in different time-frames."

All Healing is Self-healing

The client needs to understand that because their Inner Child is trapped in the event that caused it to form, it doesn't have access to the resources available to the client *now*. It only has the resources that were available at the time of the stressful event. Adult Consciousness has considerably more history and experience to draw upon. As a result, the client can provide the maturity, wisdom, and strength needed to transform the Child's experience into a learning experience. This is what allows the past to finally be the past. For example,

> "All healing is self-healing. When the time comes, your job will be to help your younger self by reviewing and re-evaluating the situation that has everything to do with what's causing the problem. Understand?

> "You can do that because you and the Child are the same person. You're just in different timeframes. Until then, just stay curious because, through the process, you will discover the thoughts and feelings of the Child you once were. Then you can transform them. When that happens, you will begin to experience dramatic change for the better in your life.

> "This is because the Child is really just your younger self. You are the Child, all grown up, now. Back then, you didn't know what you know now. You're older and wiser than you were, then. Whether you realize it or not, you have everything you need, right now, to change your life for the better. It's because you and the Child share the same feelings. When the Child feels better, you'll feel better. That's where we want to keep the focus, at all times—the feeling."

Focus On the Feeling

Some clients expect regression to be a 3D visual experience. This misconception needs to be corrected during your pre-talk because seeing is not a requirement for regression. The only thing you're interested in is the feeling. You need to keep the client focused on feelings and sensations in the body because that is the foundation for all other sensory input. When you guide a client back into a traumatic experience in the past, you want them to step into the experience and revivify the details. If the client tries to see, imagine, or consciously remember a past event, the conscious effort will prevent the recall of the repressed aspects of the memory. That's what's calling for resolution.

To revivify an event means that the client will see what they saw—*at that time.* They'll hear what they heard—*at that time.* They'll feel what they felt and know what they knew—*at that time.* Memory is stored according to how the experience was recorded the first time. This has everything to do with the age of the Child. For example, if the client regresses to infancy, awareness will be more focused on physical sensations because this is an infant's primary sensory input channel.

As a child grows and develops more auditory or visual acuity, these impressions will become more evident in your regression sessions. But they're not necessary. What's most important is the client's first impression because the first impression is always the feeling in the body. For example,

> "The Subconscious Mind doesn't speak the language of reason and logic. It speaks the language of feelings. The way it communicates with the Conscious Mind is through images and emotions.

"Emotions are felt as sensations in the body. We either feel warm and expansive or tight and constricted. A thought, on the other hand, is how we picture something in our minds. Dog. Cat. Fire. Pizza. You can form a picture in your Mind because it's coming out of memory.

"Some people expect regression to be like it's a 3D movie. But that's seldom the case. It's not about seeing. The only thing we're interested in is the feeling.

"This is a body-centered approach to healing. It's based on the idea that the body is the Subconscious Mind. When stuff happens that we don't like, we experience uncomfortable feelings—in the body. That's where we want to keep the focus—on what's happening in the body—because the body will show us where we need to go to find the healing.

"'That feeling' is a signal coming out of the event that originally caused it. It's Subconscious communication that will lead us back to the root cause of the problem.

"What you need to know is that feelings naturally arise and pass away—when we *let* them. They're like the weather. If you don't like a feeling, give it a minute. Let it express. Give yourself permission to feel the feeling, and it will pass. When it's finished, you'll start to feel better right away. You may even be surprised at how quickly it will pass when you just feel the feeling. Most people don't know this, but even the most intense feeling won't last more than 90-seconds—if you just let yourself feel it.

"An emotion is a biochemical event in the body. It's there for a reason. Emotions motivate us to take action to get our needs met. They're there to take care of us. An uncomfortable feeling is the Subconscious Mind telling you there *is* a problem. That's good. But most of us learned pretty early on to ignore or avoid uncomfortable feelings. We learned to *not* pay attention to what the Subconscious Mind is trying to tell us. That's a problem because, when you resist a feeling, it has nowhere to go. It gets trapped inside. And when a feeling gets stuck inside, it keeps trying to find a way out. It keeps trying to express. But it can't. With no way out, the pressure starts to build up inside. That can get pretty uncomfortable!

"It can start to feel like an emotional pressure-cooker inside. Well, eventually, something's got to give. 'That feeling' is going to find a way to express. It does so through symptoms. How long it takes for the symptoms to appear really depends on how much internal pressure there is. But the more pressure there is inside, the sooner the problem will make itself known on the outside."

Trauma

Everything we work with in regression sessions is essentially trauma. Big-T trauma is what most people think of as a traumatic experience—for example, surviving a serious car accident, being the victim of a rape, or witnessing violence. While these more dramatic types of experiences can be resolved through Regression Hypnotherapy, most of the time, you're going to be dealing with small-t trauma. That's where something happened, it was perceived as a threat, and it generated a stress response. As a result, the memory stuck. Clients need to know this. For example,

"Most people think trauma has to be some big, hairy-scary event but, most of the time, it's not. Trauma is simply the perception of threat while in a state of helplessness. Helplessness is the natural state of a child. And small things can feel overwhelming to a child. But often, the problem turns out to be no big deal.

"If only I had a dollar for every time a client said, 'That's it? That's what was causing the problem?' But this is what we find, most of the time. Something happens, it's unexpected, or it comes on suddenly and, because it feels like it's too much, it registers as a threat. This generates the stress response, which sends a shock throughout the nervous system of the body. That's what makes the event memorable. So, it sticks.

"Remember, the Subconscious Mind makes no distinction between a real and an imagined threat. It doesn't have to be an actual threat. It has to do with not being prepared for what was about to happen or not being psychologically equipped to deal with the situation *at that time*. By definition, that's trauma.

"Everybody's got trauma from their past. If you came into life through the womb, you've got trauma. For example, birth is inherently traumatic. Most of the time, it's not life-threatening. But children lack the maturity to be able to make sense of situations in life. That's the problem.

"The *Adult* Mind may think that what happened is no big deal, but it put the Child into a state of overwhelm. The problem is that it didn't get resolved. That's when the person stays stuck in the pattern."

The client needs to understand that it's not what happened that's the problem. It's how the Child interpreted what was happening that's causing the problem. This has everything to do with the age of the Child. For example,

> "A Child is being left at daycare for the first time is hardly life-threatening. But all the Child knows is that Mom is leaving him with a stranger. If the Child interprets this as being abandoned, it registers as a trauma. Every Child instinctively knows that if they're abandoned, they won't survive. They'll *die*. That makes the situation a very real threat. The problem is that the Child doesn't know that Mom's coming back or that the stranger they're being left with is safe. This can seed a lifelong issue.

> "Here's another example. Mummy and Daddy are having an argument. The Child is picking up on the tension between the parents. But she doesn't know how to make sense of what's happening. This makes the situation a threat to the Child.

> "The problem is that the parents aren't focused on the needs of the Child. They're focused on their own problems. But the Child doesn't understand this. What's happening just confuses the Child. When you can't figure out what's happening, that's a threat to survival. When you can't predict what's going to happen next, you don't know how to respond. This results in the Child being acutely aware of just how vulnerable they are. This is the most basic fear.

> "All the Child knows is that what's going on between Mom and Dad is distressing. It feels threatening. The Child doesn't understand that grownups have problems or that what's going for Mom and Dad are not the Child's problem. But what often

follows is that the Child will interpret this to mean, '*I'm* the problem.' The child might decide, 'It's my *fault* Mommy and Daddy are arguing. I did something wrong.' That's guilt."

"Worse, the Child could decide, 'I'm not wanted' or 'My being here is the problem.' This is because children personalize everything. They make decisions based on erroneous or partial information, which can impact a person for the rest of their life. It's all because nobody was attending to their needs as a child."

Be Transparent

Do I share this stuff with clients? Hell, yes! The Therapeutic Relationship is a partnership, an alliance. The client must be prepared to do the work necessary to achieve their Therapeutic Goal. You can't do it for them. Your job is to work *with* the Subconscious Mind. The Subconscious Mind's primary need is safety. The worst thing you could do is to make what you do a mystery.

Teach your clients how to work with you. Make what you're going to be asking them to do safe and reasonable. Satisfy the Conscious Mind's need to understand while demonstrating to the Subconscious Mind that it's safe to let you guide the process by customizing your pretalk to each client's specific needs and concerns. Speak directly to the client's presenting issue. That's what they're paying you for!

Make the client a partner in their own healing process by making your pre-talk a conversation rather than a presentation. Remember, you're going to guide the client's Adult Mind back into painful past events. You're going to be asking them to step into the event and be a support for the Child they once were.

Teach the client that it's their job to take responsibility for meeting the needs of their Inner Child. Doing so allows them to finally get their needs met as an adult.

All Trauma Isn't Bad

Traumatic experiences are a fact of life. What the client needs to understand is that all trauma isn't bad. The fundamental problem in childhood is one of dependency. The Child is dependent upon grownups to meet its needs. Whoever was responsible for doing that didn't do their job. The Child needed someone there to provide safety and help them make sense of the world of people and things around them. That didn't happen. As a result, it registered as a traumatic experience.

You can set up for the Inner Child Work during your educational pre-talk by reframing painful past events as learning opportunities. For example,

> "All trauma isn't bad. What a person learns from a traumatic experience is supposed to make them smarter, more capable, and, therefore, more likely to survive. For example, if you touched the stove and got burned, you know not to do that again, right? This ability to learn from our experiences develops what's called 'resilience.'

> "Take Forrest Gump, for example. He experienced more than a fair share of traumatic experiences—everything from shaming, bullying, to surviving a war zone and riding out a hurricane—but his childhood balanced traumatic experiences with loving support. This is what enabled him to spring back whenever life knocked him down. Human beings can spring back from traumatic experiences. When the feelings associated

with a painful or frightening situation don't get fully experienced or expressed, the emotions of the event get trapped in the memory. The Subconscious Mind then retains that memory as a current event because, as far as it's concerned, it's still happening.

"This is the trademark of trauma. Subconsciously, it's not over yet. That's how a person can end up trapped in the fears and insecurities of the Child. Even though they're all grown up now, their Subconscious Mind doesn't get that because there's a Part of them that's still stuck in a past event, trying to figure their way out of the situation.

"This is why it can sometimes feel like a two-year-old is running your life. It's because the Subconscious Mind doesn't keep time the way the Conscious Mind does. It doesn't know that *it's over.* It's still stuck there, trying to come up with a solution using the understanding of the Child at that age. The Child can't figure a way out because it only has the resources of a child.

"The way to change that is to locate the moment of decision that locked in the pattern. This is what we call the Initial Sensitizing Event (ISE). It's the first time the Child experienced that particular situation of threat. Dr. Robert Scaer[10] is a psychologist, neurologist, and world-renowned expert on trauma. He calls the ISE an event of 'kindling.'"

The Cause of the Problem

The client needs to recognize that the symptoms can be physical, or mental, or emotional, but they're the result of a problem that has been

---

[10] Author of the book, *The Body Bears the Burden: Trauma, Dissociation, and Disease.*

building up in the Subconscious over time, decades often. The good news is that if you can find the causal event, you can pull the plug on the whole pattern. For example,

"The first time is just where the problem got started. Scaer discovered that when a kindling event is left unresolved, it can set a person up for problems later in life. It's when the 'kindling' ignites that you experience symptoms. This is because subsequent events can act as reminders of the original traumatic experience. When that happens, it triggers the underlying, unresolved pattern, making it stronger. All it takes is sufficient repetition, and the whole shebang will burst into flames as the symptoms.

"Most people can't remember the first time because traumatic memories contain uncomfortable emotions, and children lack the maturity to make sense of their experiences accurately. For this reason, the ISE tends to be located some time before the age of five or six. That's the time in life when a person is the most vulnerable. Before this age, the Mind is wide open to learning. The Child is downloading information directly from the environment.

"It's all happening unconsciously. For example, by seven weeks in-utero, the entire sensory system of the body is completely developed. Think about that! The Child is downloading information direct from her environment. That's Mom!"

Memory Is Not Fact

The client also needs to understand that regression does not reveal truth or fact. Our earliest memories are based on the impressions and interpretations made by a child who lacks the ability to think critically. For example,

> "While this ability to learn unconsciously has given us an evolutionary edge, it also causes us problems. These "learnings" acquired early in life lay the foundation for our belief system.

> "Our beliefs decide what we're going to get in life. The problem is that many of our beliefs are not based on truth or fact. The logic centers of the brain are not fully developed until around age twelve. As a result, our beliefs are not always logical or rational. After all, as children, we believed in Santa Claus, the Easter Bunny, and the Tooth Fairy, right?

> "Memory is not a factual account of an event. It's a recording of impressions that got stored, for future reference, to ensure that we'd know how to respond in the future, should something like that ever happen again. All we can know, for certain, is that stuff happened in childhood. Things were said, things were done, and certain things were modeled to us early in life. Based on these things, we formed opinions about what to expect from life. But these decisions were often based on incomplete information and partial understanding.

> "The Subconscious Mind doesn't think, so it can't discriminate. It just holds onto our memories. That means that it knows where the problem is coming from. It knows how it got started

and what's causing the problem. All we need to do is *ask* it to tell us its Story. Once you know how the problem got started, you can change the whole Story.

"The reason you can change it is that that's all it is—a Story. It's a Story you've been telling yourself, over and over, again, in the privacy of your own Mind."

Summary

Linear time is a construct of the Conscious Mind. It helps us to organize events and make sense of our experiences. But the Subconscious Mind doesn't keep track of time the same way as the Conscious Mind. The Subconscious Mind is very much in the Now.

All healing is self-healing. The client does all the work. When the time comes, the client's job will be to review and re-evaluate the situation from a more mature point of view. You will then guide them to transform the thoughts and feelings of their Inner Child.

Regression requires revivification, not seeing. The foundation for all sensory input is physical sensations. The place to keep the focus is on feelings in the body.

Everyone has unresolved trauma from Childhood. But trauma doesn't have to be the big, hairy, scary deal most people think it is. Most of the time, it's little stuff. Memory is not a factual account of an event. Regression does not reveal the truth or facts about what happened. It reveals how an event was experienced at a specific age. Recall of a past event reveals perceptions, thoughts, and feelings which made an impression and formed the basis of beliefs.

Be transparent about what you do. Don't make it a mystery. Make the client a partner in their healing process by teaching them how to work with you. Satisfy Conscious and Subconscious needs by making what you will be instructing the client to do safe and reasonable.

Symptoms, whether physical, mental, or emotional, result from an unresolved problem that has been building up in the Subconscious Mind over time. The goal is to find the event that caused the problem. This is called the Initial Sensitizing Event (ISE) or event of kindling.

Conventional medicine is the medicine of WHAT – what disease, what pill. Functional medicine is the medicine of WHY – why is this symptom occurring now and, in this way, . . . what's at the root. ~**Dr. Mark Hyman**

CHAPTER 7:
Healing the Feeling

Y ou need your clients to be very aware of their feelings because feelings give you a Bridge to the past. The problem is that most people aren't very aware of their feelings because they learned, early in life, to avoid uncomfortable feelings and emotions. This tendency to avoid feelings and emotions can show up as resistance in your sessions. Teaching your clients how to find and release uncomfortable feelings during the educational pre-talk will give you a more cooperative client to work with. Proving to the client that it's possible to feel better will increase their faith in your ability to help them get some relief. Not only will this make your job easier, but it can also save valuable time when you most need it during a regression session.

As one surprised client stated, "This stuff works!"

Releasing an uncomfortable emotion can bring the client rapid relief. This begins by making it safe for your clients to allow feelings and emotions to be a part of the healing process. Begin by teaching the client that emotions like fear, anger, and sadness are felt in the body. This teaches the client to work *with* the Subconscious Mind.

The Subconscious Mind is the emotional Mind. Emotions are felt in the body. That's where the focus of attention needs to be at all times—on the body because that's how the Subconscious Mind communicates with the Conscious Mind. It does so through physical sensations.

Feelings don't just come out of nowhere. The client may not always be consciously aware of it, but there's always a thought behind every uncomfortable feeling. Feelings come in response to what we're thinking. This understanding can help a client to realize that they're not out of control of their emotions. Emotional responses to situations in daily life are not irrational. They have everything to do with a person's thoughts. For example,

> "Where do we feel our feelings? In the body, right? The body *is* the Subconscious Mind.[11] It doesn't use logic or reason, or even words, for that matter. It communicates through feelings and sensations *in the body*. This is why we want to keep the focus on the body. It's where we feel all our feelings.
>
> "Whenever we have a thought, there's going to be a corresponding feeling. A positive experience will generate positive thoughts, which express through pleasant emotions like love and acceptance.

---

[11] Candace Pert, author of *Molecules of Emotion*, gave an amazing lecture called, "Your Body is Your Subconscious Mind." This talk is available on Amazon and is highly relevant to the practice of regression hypnotherapists. The body really is the Subconscious Mind!

"Positive feelings feel good. We experience them as pleasant sensations of comfort, safety, relaxation. These feelings tend to be gentle and flowing sensations. A bad experience, on the other hand, will generate negative thoughts, which result in uncomfortable emotions like fear, anger, sadness, etc.

"Negative emotions like fear, anger, and guilt feel bad because they generate uncomfortable physical sensations like tension and pressure. These tend to express in the gut, chest, or throat areas. We want to pay particular attention to those feelings because that's the Subconscious Mind communicating.

"We all came into this life naturally programmed to be healthy and happy. Our primary drive, as human beings, is to seek pleasure and avoid pain. In other words, to feel good and avoid feeling bad. The essential goal of healing is to restore a person's ability to feel good physically, mentally, and emotionally. The problem is that most of us were taught to avoid our feelings. We were taught to *not* feel our feelings. As a result, instead of allowing our feelings to express, we learned to deny or ignore our feelings.

"Instead of permitting ourselves to express our emotions, we learned to STOP our feelings. We stuffed them down inside and put a lid on them. That's when the trouble got started. With nowhere to go, the feelings got trapped in the energy system of the body. Therapies like acupuncture, acupressure, and Meridian Tapping Techniques like EFT recognize this. They focus on releasing blocks from the energy system of the body.

"If you can feel it, you can heal it![12] Releasing emotional energy that's been trapped inside is what allows healing to happen. When you release a feeling, it creates space for newer, better energies to flow back into you. All that's needed to release a block is to feel the feeling. That's it.

"When you feel a feeling fully, you feel better, right away, because it creates space for a better feeling to flow in to replace it. It happens automatically because our natural state is one of health and happiness. It might come as a feeling of relief, peace, happiness, gratitude, or relaxation. But it's a good feeling. That's the feeling that was being blocked by holding onto the uncomfortable feeling.

"Feeling the feeling allows the feeling to express. When the expression is complete, the feeling gets to finish. Then, it's over. Relief flows in, right away, to replace it. When you feel that relief flowing into you, it tells you two things.

"First, it tells you that you have just let something go.

"Second, it tells you that you're coming back into alignment with your natural state. That's healing."

Even when we cannot see the gold, the light and love of our true nature cannot be dimmed, tarnished, or erased. ~ **Tara Birch**

---

[12] The book by John Gray, *What You Feel, You Can Heal: A Guide for Enriching Relationships* is an incredibly empowering suggestion that you can give your clients.

The Secret to Rapid Relief

The secret to proving to the client how rapidly they can experience relief lies in the Universal Healing Steps.[13] These four steps are truly universal as they apply to any healing intervention, whether it's physical, emotional, mental, or energetic. This gives you a simple, versatile protocol you can use at every phase of the healing process.

1. Find It

The first step is to find the feeling. Allowing the client to talk about the problem is often all that's needed to bring an uncomfortable feeling to awareness. Focusing attention on "that feeling" will increase awareness of the feeling, allowing more of it to come to awareness. That's what we want.

2. Feel It

In order to find the feeling, the client has to feel the feeling. Allowing the feeling to be there will empower the client to change how they feel. Teach the client to keep their focus on what's happening in the body. Invite them to notice any discomfort there. Any tightness, tension, or pressure—especially in the throat, chest, or tummy region—can be evidence of an emotion trying to express. To ensure that the client doesn't feel self-conscious, let them know that, should you notice something, you're going to mention it so they can bring their attention to it. Then, as you proceed, keep your attention on the client's body. Watch carefully for signs of tension or tightness, body twitching, chewing a lip, grimacing, etc. Teach your client how to recognize Subconscious Communication. For example,

---

[13] You can learn more in *The Devil's Therapy: Hypnosis Practitioner's Essential Guide to Effective Regression Hypnotherapy.*

"We want to stay focused on what's happening in the body. That's the Subconscious Mind speaking. And we're here to listen. What this means is that any tension or tightness, any discomfort, whatsoever, we want to pay attention to that. We're not here to judge. We're here to listen. If I happen to notice something—for example, some twitching or tension— I'm going to ask you about it because you may not be aware of it. I want you to **be very aware of what's happening in the body**, okay, because that's how your Subconscious Mind communicates. Understand?"

3. Heal It

Once the client is able to find a feeling in the body, the next step is to name "that feeling." That's what's calling for healing. What you're after is the actual emotion associated with that specific sensation in the body. Don't assume you know what it might be. It's the client's job to find the feeling and then name the emotion that trying to express. The client could be experiencing a scared feeling, or an angry feeling, or something else. You won't know what it is until the client tells you what it is. For example,

> "If that tense, tight feeling in the throat were an emotion, what would it be?"

Teach your client how to avoid using labels. Words like stressed, upset, anxious, and worried are not emotions. They're a way of avoiding the emotion that's trying to express by getting some distance from it. Saying, "I feel upset," may be a socially acceptable way to express how you're feeling, but it's a way of getting some distance from a feeling you just don't like. Avoiding is a real problem, and it won't help you get to the root cause of the problem.

You need to teach your clients to identify authentic emotions such as scared, afraid, angry, mad, sad. These are feelings that can be felt and released to bring relief. When a person lets themselves feel the feeling in the body and then names the authentic emotion associated with that feeling, it starts to lose its power. That's when it becomes safe to claim the feeling as their own. For example, "This scared feeling in my heart" or "This angry feeling in my gut."

> *Why do you stay in prison when the door is so wide open? Move outside the tangle of fear-thinking. The entrance door to the sanctuary is inside you.*
>
> ~ Rumi

When a client becomes aware of a feeling inside, that's their feeling. But if they don't claim it as their own, they can't do anything with it. They're powerless to the feeling. When the client takes ownership of the feeling, they claim their power of choice. Now they can decide what they want to do with it. They can choose to hold onto the feeling, or they can let it go. This empowers the client to begin feeling better right away.

An easy way to claim a feeling is with autosuggestion.[14] Simply have the client say it out loud. "I feel angry!" Or, "I feel sad." Or "I feel scared." Autosuggestion is a powerful technique to use in your sessions because it gets the client doing the work of self-healing. It is much more powerful than direct suggestion because when clients say something out loud, they give *themselves* a suggestion.

---

[14] Autosuggestion is directed self-talk developed by Emile Coue at the beginning of the twentieth century. It was Coue who coined the famous affirmation, "Every day, in every way, I'm getting better and better."

This is not a suggestion that the client can either choose to accept or reject. It's a suggestion they can feel the truth of. If the client feels angry, saying, "I feel angry" is a statement of truth. The client can feel the truth of these words. Speaking the truth of how you feel is an act of empowerment that helps make it safe for the client to give the angry feeling permission to be there. Allowing the feeling to be there is taking ownership of the feeling. It's claiming the feeling.

When a person tells themselves something that isn't true, they can feel it. It will feel kind of "off." There will be a response in the body that feels like resistance or tension. That's the body saying "no." Or "false." Or "wrong." This valuable feedback tells the client what is true at a Subconscious level of Mind.

This gives you an effective tool for gauging the acceptability of a suggestion before you ever deliver it. If it feels true, the suggestion is acceptable. It's believable. If it feels off or generates tension, there's resistance to that suggestion. It's not believable or true. Check it out for yourself. Say something that you know isn't true. For example, "My name is Marilyn Monroe."

As you say these words, notice how it feels in the body. If you felt a little twinge or tightness in your gut, tension in your throat, or discomfort in your chest, realize that your BS[15] detector just went off. Try saying this one: "I am rich."

Are you beginning to you recognize what an amazingly accurate feedback system this gives you access to? Think about how being able to test the acceptability of a suggestion in session might help to improve your results! All you need to do is ask a client to say something

---

[15] BS stands for Belief System

out loud and notice how it feels to say those words. If it feels good, it must be true. If it feels off, that's resistance. Resistance tells you that there's a block. Something about that suggestion is not true.

Sometimes, the resistance will be really obvious. The client will have trouble speaking. They'll stumble over their words or mispronounce them. The words will get stuck in the throat. Some clients will choke on the words. Alternately, the resistance could be more subtle. For example, the client might notice a slight churning sensation in their gut or a flutter in their heart—the stronger the feeling, the stronger the resistance.

The key to understanding this marvelous biological feedback system we have all been given is how it feels. If it doesn't feel good, the Subconscious Mind is telling us that the suggestion is not acceptable. It's coming into conflict with an established belief. This is why affirmations can actually make a problem worse. If telling yourself, "I'm smart," and "I'm wealthy," is setting off your alarm system, guess what? Repeating that suggestion is going to reinforce the internal resistance to it. If there's only slight resistance, you might be able to override a negative belief through repetition. That's when affirmations can work. But if there's a strong negative response to a suggestion, repeating it will increase the resistance. It will compound the negative response making the problem worse.

It's all about congruence. The client may say, "I accept myself" or "I forgive you," but how does it *feel* to say those words. If the client's BS detector is going off, there's a Subconscious block. Get to work and release it!

4. Seal It

The final step is to prove that it's possible to feel better by teaching your client how to release the uncomfortable feeling. Of course, the method you choose will depend on the releasing techniques you currently have available to you. In some cases, autosuggestion alone can be very effective. Just speaking the truth of how you feel can bring an immediate sense of relief because it's no longer a dirty little secret trapped inside the mind-body system. I like to use tapping[16] because it's simple and quick.

Many of us spend our whole lives running from feeling with the mistaken belief that you can not bear the pain. But you have already borne the pain. What you have not done is feel all you are beyond that pain. ~ **Kahlil Gibran**

Tapping Techniques

Tapping is a versatile tool that can be used at every phase of the healing process. It's an especially valuable tool for use in Regression Hypnotherapy sessions because it gives you a way to quickly and easily release stuck emotions. As a result, tapping can really help to move things along in a regression session. If you don't know how to tap, this is a tool worth acquiring. It's easy to learn, and you can teach a client how to tap and release an uncomfortable emotion in just a few minutes. This is also an incredibly powerful tool when combined with Regression Hypnotherapy.

---

[16] Tapping is the general term used to describe Meridian Tapping Techniques based on Emotional Freedom Technique (EFT).

A Preliminary Technique

Some clients have doubts or concerns about hypnosis. If the client feels a little apprehensive, you can use tapping during your pre-talk to neutralize the fear. If the client feels overwhelmed, confused, or frustrated, you can reduce the overall volume of internal pressure. Releasing fear, doubt, and frustration before you begin the hypnosis means the client won't be carrying those things into the hypnosis session. This reduces the amount of resistance that you have to deal with. Much easier.

A Convincer

It only takes a few minutes to teach a person how to tap. In just a few rounds of tapping, you can show the client how quickly and easily they can shift to a better feeling. Any shift toward the better can then be used as evidence that change is possible. There's no better Convincer than proof! Prove that you can help the client to feel better, and they will be less inclined to question you or the process. Instead, they'll be looking forward to the benefits of change.

An Induction

Tapping combines focused attention and suggestion. That's hypnosis. During the tapping sequence, the client focuses on a feeling in the body while tapping on the points and speaking aloud. This acts as a Confusion Induction while giving you a very organic approach to quickly (and covertly) induce a state of hypnosis.

A Bridge

During a Tapping sequence, thoughts and feelings will naturally bubble up to the surface of awareness. Any feeling is potentially a Bridge to the past. The stronger the feeling, the stronger the Bridge. As soon as a client starts to experience a strong emotion, you have a Bridge that you can follow back into the event that caused it. As a result, tapping can be used as a launchpad for Regression to Cause. Just bring up the feeling and count the client back into a scene from the past. Easy-peezy!

A Spontaneous Regression

The Mind works through association. As the client focuses on thoughts, feelings, and sensations in the body, their Mind will naturally associate with earlier situations when the client felt that way. This can lead to a spontaneous regression—the best kind!

A Releasing Technique

Virtually everything we work with in Regression Hypnosis is based on some kind of traumatic experience. Tapping has been proven to be effective for resolving traumatic memory because it calms the amygdala. The amygdala is the brain's alarm center that is responsible for generating the fight or flight response. If you turn off the alarm, the client will go back to feeling safe and secure, calm and relaxed. That's when healing happens.

Tapping allows you to quickly release the emotional charge that's been holding the problem in place. As the client releases the emotions that got trapped in an event, they experience rapid relief. This can help to clear the path to the ISE.

When you tap on feelings in a past event, there are often layers of perceptions, thoughts, and feelings. Clearing one layer will give you access to the next, deeper level. In this way, you can grind down to the root cause of the client's presenting issue. If you clear *all* the aspects contributing to the problem, you'll get complete healing. This really is the key to getting a lasting result.

During your pre-talk, teach your clients that it's okay for them to follow your instructions to tap and talk while feeling a feeling. If you don't, the client may think it's weird and hold back during a session. Make it safe and normal to do what you're going to ask them to do. For example,

> "There are three things human beings naturally do. First, we touch ourselves. If you bang your shin or elbow, what do you do? You rub it, right? We touch the 'owie' or get Mom to kiss it better.

> "The second thing human beings do naturally is—we feel feelings. Where do you feel your feelings? In the body, right? That's where we want to focus attention—on what's happening in the body.

> "The third thing we do is talk to ourselves in the privacy of our own minds. Unfortunately, some of the things we say to ourselves aren't all that nice. And some of the things we say are just downright nasty!

> "The things we say to ourselves, about ourselves, in the privacy of our own Mind affect how we feel. When we say unkind or untrue things, it generates tension and tightness in the body that can cause pain.

> "What we're going to do is use these three things that we do *naturally*—touching, feeling, and talking—to release stressful feelings from the body so that you can feel better. Okay?"

With the client's permission, you can now invite them to follow along as you teach them how to talk and tap. Follow the four Universal Healing Steps—find it, feel it, heal it, seal it! As the client talks about the problem, have them tap while focusing on what's happening in the body.

1. Find it

Notice the feeling that comes up in the body. Give it permission to be there. For example, "Stay focused on that feeling. That's the Subconscious Mind communicating. That feeling has everything to do with (the problem)."

2. Feel it

Guide the client to name the emotion they're feeling in the body. For example, "Say, I feel . . . what emotion? Sad, mad, glad, scared, or something else?"

3. Heal it

As the client continues to focus on the feeling in the body, guide them to claim the feeling while tapping on the points. For example, "I feel angry. I'm allowed to feel this angry." Or, "I feel sad. I'm allowed to feel this sad."

4. Seal it

Practice a round or two of releasing the feeling. Then ask the client to notice what, if anything, has changed. Even a slight shift can be used as proof that change is possible. This means that, in just a few minutes, you can show the client that it's possible to get relief working with you.

Teaching your clients how to work with you during the pre-talk will reduce resistance and increase client motivation, giving you a better client when it comes to doing the hypnosis. Not only does this give you a client who knows how to work with their own biological feedback system, but it also gives you a way to test whether or not an issue has been truly resolved. How do you know for sure? They'll feel it.

This gives you a client who knows how to:

- Focus on feelings in the body.
- Allow themselves to feel their feelings.
- Name the emotion expressed through the feeling.
- Tap to release the emotion.

Not only that, in just a few minutes, you will have taught your client to follow your instructions. They'll have experienced what it means to take responsibility for their feelings. They'll have learned that it's safe to let themselves allow uncomfortable emotions to come to awareness. And they'll know that it's possible to feel better. That's pretty good mileage for a simple technique, right?

A Homework Assignment

Tapping is a great way to empower your clients between sessions. It literally gives them relief at their fingertips. Once you have taught your client how to tap and you're confident that they're ready to use it on their own, you can assign it as homework.

Make sure that the client is willing to practice on their own before you assign homework. A client who is willing to do homework between sessions gives you a much better client to work with. This is someone who is participating in their healing. But if there's resistance to homework, don't require it. While tapping between sessions can accelerate the healing, it's not a requirement for the client to successfully work with you.

A Self-Healing Strategy

Tapping on your own issues can teach you a great deal about the healing process. For example, you'll discover how tapping naturally induces a light state of hypnosis. You're tapping into the Subconscious Mind. You can discover for yourself how releasing the surface layers of an issue can free up deeper layers to be released. You can even self-regress and experience how the Mind naturally associates with earlier events by connecting to thoughts, feelings, and sensations related to an issue you're working on.

You'll discover how regression happens very naturally. All that's needed to regress into an event is the willingness to let it happen. This means that you can do your own work of self-healing. You can self-regress to resolve past events using the same tools and techniques you use with clients. This will give you a deeper understanding of how your therapeutic tools and techniques work. All in all, tapping is a very useful tool for you to have in your therapeutic toolkit. But like every tool, it requires skill to use effectively.

Additional Releasing Techniques

Many hypnosis practitioners started with technique-based methods like Neuro-Linguistic Programming (NLP) or Emotional Freedom Tapping (EFT). What brought them into Regression Hypnosis was a desire to do healing work. If you already know how to do tapping, you'll find that combining it with Regression to Cause will give you a powerful strategy for resolving the root cause of a client's problem. If you're new to tapping, focus on mastering the tools of Regression

Hypnosis before adding anything to it. Then, once you're confident in your abilities to facilitate Regression Hypnotherapy effectively, add tapping to it to achieve deeper healing.

Remember, the key to releasing trapped emotions lies in keeping the focus on the feeling in the body. Feeling the feeling fully will allow the feeling to finish. Speaking out loud while moving the body helps to move the feeling out. Get it out, and it's over.

The following alternative releasing techniques can also be taught very easily during the educational pre-talk. Like tapping, they only take a few minutes to teach and can dramatically improve your results by getting your client participating in their healing process.

Karate Chop Point

The karate chop point is located on the fleshy part of the side of the hand. Have the client focus on a thought or a feeling and tap on the point while speaking the truth of that feeling.

Neuro-lymphatic Release Points

Neuro-lymphatic release points are the sore spots on either side of the upper chest. Just poke around a little to find them. Then rub gently on these points while speaking the truth about the feeling.

Collarbone Point

The collarbone point is located on the inner edge of the collarbone. Place your fingers on the bumps on either side of the throat. Then move an inch or two from the center along the collarbone. You'll feel a slight indentation. Gently tap or rub on this point.

Bi-lateral Tapping

Bi-lateral tapping helps balance the hemispheres of the brain. It's a self-soothing technique that anyone can use. Have the client hug themselves by crossing their arms across their chest, with the hands on their upper part of the arms, alternate tapping on the left and right sides.

Pillow Therapy

Pillow Therapy is the mainstay of emotional release work in Regression Hypnotherapy. This is an especially helpful technique when you're releasing those bigger, hairy-scary feelings like fear and anger. Guide the client to focus on the feeling while pumping it into the pillow. This gives the feeling a place to go so that the client doesn't have to carry it inside anymore.

The purpose of releasing is to reduce internal resistance. One small shift toward the better for the Conscious Mind can be a giant leap of trust for the Subconscious Mind. This can increase the client's willingness to move forward. All you need to do is show the client that it's possible to feel better, and they'll start moving in the right direction.

The Feeling Test

Once the client experiences a little shift toward the better, you can conduct the following test. Ask, "Was that fear (or anger, or sadness, or whatever feeling they were feeling) . . . was that a new feeling or an old familiar feeling?" This is a question you should frequently be asking in regression sessions to test for the ISE. Why not introduce it during your educational pre-talk to teach your clients to feel the answer to a question?

Here's the trick. During your educational pre-talk, the feeling you're releasing isn't new, is it? If the client answers, "New," challenge them. There's nothing going on in your office to generate that feeling. The client brought "that feeling" in with them. This means that the correct answer, the logical answer, is "familiar." For example,

> "I don't want you to think the answer to this question. I want you to feel the answer. Just go with how the body feels because the body doesn't lie. First impression—that (fear) that you were feeling in your (gut) . . . was that a new feeling, like a surprise . . . or an old, familiar feeling like, 'oh-boy, here we go, again'? First impression—new or familiar?"

When the client answers correctly, you can plant the next little seed by suggesting that "that feeling" is connected every time they feel that way. That's where you plan to take them in the regression work. Remind the client that they have a whole history with that feeling. For example,

> "That feeling" goes all the way back to the first time you ever felt that way. That's when that feeling was 'new.' The goal is to get to the first time and heal it there."

Summary

Teaching your clients how to find and release uncomfortable feelings during the educational pre-talk can give you a more cooperative client. Proving to the client that it's possible to feel better will increase their faith in your ability to help them get some relief.

Teach your clients how to work with the Subconscious Mind by focusing on feelings and sensations in the body. As the Subconscious Mind is the feeling Mind, that's where the client's attention needs to be focused. Uncomfortable emotions such as fear, sadness, and anger are felt in targeted areas of the torso—for example, the gut, chest, or throat.

Human beings naturally seek pleasure and avoid pain. But when we avoid a feeling, it has nowhere to go. When feelings get trapped in the body, they generate painful blocks. Make it safe for the client to allow emotions to be part of the healing process by teaching them how to release uncomfortable feelings. Releasing the block brings rapid relief.

Teaching your client how to find, feel, and claim a feeling to release it is a way to empower your clients while building confidence in the healing process. Once the client knows how to find, feel, claim and release a feeling to feel better, you can introduce the Feeling Test. Teach the client to feel the answer to a question and recognize when a feeling is new or familiar

The four Universal Healing steps are very versatile and can be combined with any releasing techniques you might use. For example, you could combine this with tapping or EFT, Pillow Therapy, breathwork, or just use it on its own as a way to express feelings verbally.

Autosuggestion is a powerful tool that you can use in your sessions that gives you a way to test the acceptability of your suggestions. You can use it to test the truth of a suggestion while teaching the client that they can trust their feelings and, as a result, themselves. That's huge.

Tapping Techniques are very effective when combined with Regression Hypnotherapy. If you don't yet know tapping, there are many alternative techniques you can use to release trapped emotions from the body's energy system.

CHAPTER 8:
Contract for Healing

O n May 5, 1976, Dana Ullman, America's leading spokesperson for homeopathy, was arrested for practicing medicine without a license. Ullman's lawyer, Jerry Green, was a malpractice attorney and bodyworker who discovered that a significant contributor to malpractice claims stemmed from people expecting more than doctors could provide. His solution? A health contract to clearly identify the specific roles and responsibilities for the patient and practitioner in the Therapeutic Relationship.

"The old view of doctor/patient relationships was that the doctor provided the treatment, and the patient didn't do anything except to take whatever medication the doctor prescribed. However, the emerging holistic health revolution not only heralded the use of various alternative treatment methods it also strongly encouraged the person (who isn't just a "patient") to take an active role in his/her health. The use of a contract in health care was a totally new concept, though it fits in with the emerging realization that each person has a role, even a vital role, in his/her own health care."[17]

---

[17] https://www.huffpost.com/entry/when-getting-arrested-for_b_9780342

The purpose of the Therapeutic Contract for Regression Hypnotherapy is to define the Therapeutic Relationship by establishing who does what. This is what your educational pre-talk has been leading up to. The Therapeutic Contract gives you permission to do your job while making the client responsible for the results. But to agree to a Contract, the client must be able to make an informed decision.

Regression Hypnotherapy is not a passive process. It requires the client's participation. The client must be prepared to go where you need them to go and do what you need them to do to achieve the desired result. For example, you need the client's permission to induce hypnosis. You need the client to be willing to allow feelings and emotions to be a part of the process. You can't just do it for them.

Nothing is going to happen without the client's consent. The client must be willing to let you guide them and follow your instructions. For example, the client must be willing to follow your instructions to enter into a state of somnambulism because real regression requires somnambulism. To regress to the causal event, the client must be willing to allow uncomfortable feelings and emotions to come to awareness. To create the change they want, the client must be willing to face uncomfortable memories from the past and release trapped emotions.

The three Fs in Contract

The Contract for Regression Hypnotherapy has two parts.

1. Permission to allow hypnosis
2. Permission to regress to the causal event

The following three Fs establish a clearly defined Therapeutic Contract that allows both hypnosis and Regression to Cause to happen.

The first F in the Contract is FOLLOW.

The client must agree to follow your instructions. This agreement establishes compliance. You need that. This is the foundation for the Therapeutic Contract. If the client isn't willing to follow your instructions, you can't help them. Without compliance, you're going nowhere. Some hypnosis practitioners don't like the word "compliance." They think it means control. But compliance simply means cooperation.

You need the client's cooperation to resolve the cause of the problem. The client's conscious agreement to follow instructions ensures that they won't try to run your session. That's your job. In exchange, you agree to care, protect and guide them safely through the healing process. As safety is the Subconscious Mind's Prime Directive, when you take on the job of protecting the client, the Subconscious Mind will relax and let you guide the process.

The second F in the Contract is FOCUS.

The client must agree to keep the focus of attention on feelings in the body. Emotions are experienced as physical sensations in the body— primarily in the throat, chest, and gut. This is how the Subconscious Mind communicates with the Conscious Mind. But emotions like fear, anger, or sadness don't feel good. As a result, the tendency is to avoid. That's a problem. The Subconscious Mind has been communicating all along. The client hasn't been listening. You need to change that.

Maintaining focus helps to keep the client out of their head. If they start thinking, it will only get in the way of the process. The moment the client starts to think, you'll lose the signal. You'll lose the Bridge. When that happens, it is game over. You can prevent this from happening by teaching the client to stay focused on the feeling. This maintains the direct connection to the ISE. For example,

> "The only thing we're interested in is the feeling. That's the Subconscious Mind speaking. Subconsciously, the feeling is what's real. 'That feeling' is what's calling for resolution. It's a signal coming out of the event that caused it. It will guide you to the Truth. Understand?"

Some people expect regression to be a visual experience. They think they're going to step into a 3D lucid experience. This is an unrealistic expectation that needs to be corrected. How an event is recalled depends on how the memory got stored in the first place. This is based on the strongest impressions *at that time*. While the client might step into a visual or auditory experience, our primary channel for sensory input, from the earliest age, is physical sensations. That's why we want to keep the focus on feelings in the body. Remind the client that Regression Hypnosis is a highly individual experience, that it's not necessarily seeing, and the only thing you're interested in is the feeling.

The third F is FIRST.

The ISE represents the first time the client ever experienced "that feeling." The goal is to locate the ISE because this specific event contains all the details about how the client's problem got started. Once the ISE has been identified, the uncovering process focuses on identifying the specific aspects responsible for generating the symptoms. The therapeutic work then focuses on finding ways to satisfy the underlying Subconscious need for symptom expression.

To locate and resolve the real problem, the client must agree to set aside thinking and trust their first impression. This requires the client to answer quickly—not mull things over. For example,

"When I ask you a question, *don't think*. Just give me your first impression. I want you to answer quickly. Understand?"

First impressions come quickly. The problem is that they don't always make sense. As a result, the client may be tempted to question themselves. This can lead to unnecessary thinking and analysis, which will only block the uncovering process. To prevent this, inform the client that their first impression doesn't have to make sense. For example,

> "This is important. When I ask you a question, you don't think the answer, you *feel* the answer. Understand?
>
> "Thinking, analyzing, and judging is using the wrong part of the Mind. Thinking takes time. First impressions are what matter here. They come quickly because they're Subconscious responses. I want you to answer quickly. Okay?
>
> "Just let that Thinking Part of you stay off in the sidelines. If it doesn't make sense, that's okay. You can *be curious* about what might be revealed through the process. But it doesn't have to make sense because whatever comes to mind is not coming from the rational, Thinking Mind. It's coming out of the irrational, feeling part of the Mind. That's what we want.
>
> "The Subconscious Mind has its own kind of logic and reasoning. So, it doesn't have to make sense. In fact, often, it won't make sense—at least, not to begin with. The important thing is this: When I ask you a question, answer quickly. There's no need to try to figure anything out. Just go with your first impression. *Later* it will all make sense. Okay?"

Testing the three Fs in the Contract

If you've already taught the client how to release a feeling, they've already demonstrated their willingness to follow your instructions. They have also shown their willingness to focus on feelings in the body. All that's left is to test the client's ability to respond quickly during the uncovering procedure. To do that, they need to learn how to feel the answer.

Invite the client to close their eyes. Instruct them to respond to your questions with their first impression. Remind the client that there's no right or wrong answer; the only thing you're interested in is their first impression. Then, ask your client to *feel* the answer to each of the following three uncovering questions[18] of Regression Hypnotherapy. For example,

> "First impression, does it *feel* like it's daytime or nighttime? What's your first sense?
>
> "First impression, does it *feel* like you're inside or outside?
>
> "First impression, does it feel like you're alone or with someone?"

Whatever the client answers, validate it by saying, "Good!" or "Good job!" Then move on to the next question. Complete the exercise and have the client open their eyes. That's it. Remember, the only thing you're testing here is to see if the client is following your instruction to

---

[18] These are the first three of the Six Basic Uncovering Questions of Regression Hypnotherapy in *The Devil's Therapy: Hypnosis Practitioner's Essential Guide to Effective Regression Hypnotherapy.*

answer quickly with their first impression. What happens next depends on how the client responds to each question.

1. Did the client follow instructions to answer quickly?
2. Was the client focused on feeling the answer?
3. Was the client responding with their first impression?

If the answer to any of these questions is "no," recognize that the client is thinking. In this case, you need to find out what about your instructions the client did not understand. Educate them further, then repeat the test. The key to successful Regression Hypnotherapy lies in testing. Never proceed to the next step until the client successfully completes the step that you're on.

If the answer to all three questions is "yes," you have successfully established a Contract for hypnotherapy. Good job! Give yourself a pat on the back. Congratulate the client on how well they did. Then, review the instructions to reinforce the desired responses. For example,

> "That's all there is to it. When I ask you a question, give me your first impression. There's no need to think or try to figure anything out. Just give me your first sense."

If the client's answers seem incongruent, for example, it's daytime, and the client answers, "Nighttime," or you're inside with the client, and they answer, "Outside" or "Alone," you have a choice of how to proceed. If you suspect that the client has spontaneously regressed to a scene, you could dive right into the regression work. My preference is to complete the exercise. But if the client goes into a full-blown abreaction, it's a gift. Grab it and run with it! Otherwise, when they open their eyes, congratulate the client on how well they did, then casually ask, "A moment ago, your Mind had you somewhere. What happened? Where did your Mind take you?"

Summary

The Therapeutic Contract gives you permission to do your job while making the client responsible for the results. This is what your educational pre-talk has been leading up to.

The 3Fs in the Contract for Regression to Cause are:

1. Follow
2. Focus
3. First

If you have taught the client how to find, feel and release a feeling, they have already demonstrated their willingness to follow instructions and focus on feelings in the body. All that is left is to test the client's responses to the uncovering procedure.

Are they following instructions to answer quickly? Are they focused on feeling the answer? Are they responding with their first impression? If so, you have a Contract for Regression to Cause Hypnotherapy.

Good job!

CHAPTER 9:
Educational Pre-Talk for Teen Hypnotherapy

Barbara Scholl, Switzerland

Today is a good day. I just finished disposing of tissues soaked with tears and a hint of mascara left behind by my teen client, who came to see me at my hypnotherapy office this morning. This sixteen-year-old girl booked her session herself online for 9 a.m.! Pretty amazing since we can all recall that, as a teenager, 9 a.m. felt like in the middle of the night.

If an observer had seen this athletic adolescent girl walk in my office this morning, he might have wondered, "Does a girl, who is so cute, punctual, and polite, really need therapy? For what?" With these impressions, I would like to welcome you to my chapter as a guest writer for my dear friend and mentor, Wendie Webber. Be assured, the world does urgently need teen hypnotherapists. In the upcoming pages, my goal is to pass on my passion and love for teen hypnotherapy to YOU. Picture the bright torch being passed on at the Olympic Games and get ready to become a fulfilled and proud carrier of the Torch for Teen Hypnotherapy!

Join me, now, as I walk you through how I go about the Educational Pre-talk for Teen Hypnotherapy, pointing out peculiarities, stuff to watch out for, and valuable general information.

Step 1: Electronic Data Sheet Prior to the Teen Session

Usually, the parents sign up for the adolescent's therapy either by phone or directly on my online calendar. I then forward an electronic Data Sheet to them, collecting information relevant to the session in regard to family status, siblings, health issues, challenges the teen has already encountered — for example, bullying, accidents, losses, divorce of parents, medications, drug use, self-mutilation, eating disorders, and similar.

Why do I recommend gathering this information beforehand? It allows me to feel the temperature of the teen and, just as important, of the family. When working with younger kids, it makes sense that exploring the family systems matters. With teens, however, we might assume that they are almost adults and, therefore, can speak for themselves. However, some teens have been bullied, or hurt, or isolated by others. They might be too ashamed or too withdrawn to tell us the truth of their situation at home when they first come to see us. They may also block specific incidents from their memory.

Even though we gather this information before the session, we must never work in a leading or suggestive way. All we can do is keep this information in the back of our minds to facilitate putting the puzzle pieces in the desired order during the therapy session. For example, I do not approach the teen and ask him,

> "So, tell me all about being bullied in third grade by this guy from the soccer team." Instead, I pose the question, "You know what? I have a lot of teens who come in to see me who have, at some point, experienced painful bullying or isolation at school or in peer groups. Have you ever lived through difficult times like that?"

Always keep in mind that what is true for any client applies to teens, as well. The door to inner healing always opens inward. Building rapport and trust with teens is, therefore, elementary.

Step 2: Pre-Talk with Parents Present in the Room

I always start out the teen session with the parents present in the room to deliver the professional pre-talk. Why, you might wonder? This is a setting where the teen still feels "safe." This gives the parents time to check me out and see how I treat their teenager. My Pre-Talk is very dynamic, fun (convincers), and visual but, at the same time, highly professional. It is a valuable time slot in which we get to educate and inform the family about modern Regression Hypnosis.

Mind Model

I use a teen-adapted version of Gerald F. Kein's Mind Model so that they can visualize the Conscious Mind and the Subconscious Mind. Explaining how super-cool and powerful this part of their brain fascinates most adolescents. For example,

> "The Subconscious Mind is the home of your long-term memory. Everything you have ever experienced, felt, learned and perceived, is stored there. It's like a video camera that captures all of your senses. It functions very much like the hard drive of a computer. The storage capacity of this hard drive is comparable to watching Netflix for thirty years, non-stop, and everything is stored!"

It's here that I get the first jaw drop of the teen. The second follows when I explain the difference between the Conscious and Subconscious parts of the Mind. For example,

> "If you put your Conscious Mind (5-10 percent of your Mind) and your Subconscious Mind (90-95 percent of your Mind) up for a foot race/sprint, the referee shouts, 'Ready, steady, go!' Then your Conscious Mind starts to think, 'Alright, I will run in a second!' In the meantime, during these few split-seconds of thinking by the Conscious Mind, your Subconscious Mind has run 250 km/miles!"

Let me assure you, at this point, every teenager is going to be fully awake in your big, comfy therapy chair and up for more. Why? Because we meet the teen in their world. Of course, this comparison to distance is in regards to the neurons firing in the brain. We have now created an emotional state in the teen or SURPRISE and CURIOSITY. The door to inner healing has started opening up.

I further explain how the Subconscious Mind is programmed until the age of about twelve years and how limiting beliefs may sneak in during these early years. I explain to the teen that today s/he will have the opportunity to sort out the unwanted limiting beliefs, replacing them with the ones s/he chooses, and her/his desires and s/he considers best suited for her/himself. Pretty promising in the ears of a teen, do you agree? The door of inner healing opens up another bit.

Willpower

The next component I focus on is willpower. I point out to the teen— and parents must hear this too—that willpower is located on the Conscious Mind (5-10 percent of our brain), and that Willpower is highly, highly, highly, highly, highly overestimated! Willpower helps us to do something or not do something in the short run. But in the long run, it is always our programming on the hard disk of our Subconscious Mind which prevails.

What do you think happens now in the teen brain? Yes, another penny starts dropping. At this point, you can usually observe a great relief in the microbody movements of the young human being in front of you. Guilt starts to drop away because, up until now, they have tried to get rid of their problem by willpower. Their parents, teachers, and friends might have been telling them, "Come on, try harder, show some effort, struggle, strive, do it again, stretch yourself." The teen now realizes, "Oh wow, I maybe am not a complete loser, after all! Maybe I am not a total failure. Maybe this hypnotherapist can actually help me."

Did you just now get some goosebumps? I get them repeatedly, working with teens who come in hurting. As their mind, heart, and soul start opening up, they experience gratitude and relief. This is the sweet oxytocin kickback we get from facilitating teen hypnotherapy.

The door to inner healing always opens inward.

Teamwork

Hypnosis is teamwork. This is a fact I point out while the parents are still in the room because this requirement must be clear to all involved. Our job is not to fix and repair teens. Hypnotherapy is not a "erase all the negatives" pill. It is the magic of teamwork. For example,

> "Let me assure you that hypnotherapy is teamwork. It is as if we go on a jeep safari, and you are at the steering wheel. I will tell you to turn left, to turn right, to brake, to accelerate. If you do not press the gas pedal, we will not go anywhere.

> "Further, a rock on the roadside might show up, and I will ask you to lift it up and look beneath it. If you decide, 'No, I don't feel like lifting it because I do not want to look at the emotion below the rock,' then I cannot lift it up for you. Only you can do so."

This translates into the fact that I am only as good as my client allows me to be. With this metaphor, we guide our young clients into responsibility. It is not us doing it for them while they chill in the therapy chair. I tell them that I will lead them through the process today. I'm a bit like a tour guide. The work, however—and the glory for the result, as well—is all on them. It is all about self-empowerment. After the session, the teen's subconscious mind will fully understand what we meant with these words.

We meet the teen in his or her own world.

Hypnotic Convincers

During the pre-talk, you can use hypnotic convincers to demonstrate to the teen what it means to use the "power of your thoughts." This is especially useful when working with young, talented athletes who come in for an increase in performance, getting rid of mental blocks, or speeding up the healing of injuries. Dynamic hypnotic convincers allow the younger teens to get out of the chair to do fun exercises, further building rapport. I usually apply the "Gummie Bear Twist" convincer, which involves eating a sour gummy bear.

Naming the Problem by its Name

After establishing basic rapport, I pose the following question to the teen, "You know, I ask smaller kids which three wishes they would like to have come true. For example, if a fairy or Sandman came by during the night, what three wishes would they make come true?" This is a comfortable door-opener to start talking about why they came in to see me today.

The teen will often exchange eyesight with the parents when they tell me where they are hurting. I hardly ever experience mismatches between parents and teens regarding the problem to be solved. On the contrary, I experience immense gratitude from the parents that I am here to help their teenager with his/her issue. This might be the positive effect of social security not paying for child and teen hypnotherapy (at least, here in Switzerland, they do not pay yet). Because the parents must pay, a "natural selection" takes place. Parents who are willing to pay for teen hypnotherapy are highly grateful for your help.

I also have teens who come from very affluent backgrounds. One might think that their parents would demand that their kids be "fixed" according to success and high-performance criteria. These parents, however, are just as grateful, humble, and open to learning more about hypnotherapy.

It is all about self-empowerment.

No Guarantee of Success

With the parents still in the room, I also explain to the teen that, just like a doctor, I cannot give a guarantee of success. I then assure the teen that if we work together as a team, we can do magic together. I mention that while I cannot guarantee success, my office calendar is booked out for the next two months because it seems that "this stuff works!"

Today, I point out that we will do uncovering using cause-oriented regression that "teenagers experience as extremely cool." Already, I am enriching my semantics with a hint of adolescent terms—never too much, however, as it might get very cheesy! Although parents are in the room, I fully address the youngster because HE or SHE is my client.

Signature by Parents and Teen

Now the moment has come where we check to see if the teen or parents have any further questions regarding hypnosis. If all is clear, we get the parents to sign the consent form confirming that I may work with their son or daughter. I always make the adolescent sign the form, as well. This delivers an important, subliminal message that I am working with him/her.

Pretalk Alone with the Teen

I accompany the parents back to the waiting room, then spend another fifteen minutes with the teen alone before we get going with hypnosis. These few minutes, with just the two of us, are absolute magic. You will notice an immediate shift once the parents are out of the room. I find myself becoming calmer, too. My voice changes, my speed of talking slows down. I now open up my heart and soul unconditionally to the teen.

Often, I get to hear the phrase, "You won't tell my parents?" I assure the teen that nothing will leave this room and that, like a doctor, unless I suspect that a teen might harm him or herself, I am obliged to confidentiality. Now the teen and I can tune into the very confidential talk. You will hear some very touching stories. Often, teens will not have told anyone, yet, what they will share with you. You will then sense the relief in the youngster who can finally share deep sorrow, pain, or fear with a person of trust. For example,

> "My parents do not know, but I passed out the other night for two hours on the school's recreation area because I took some drugs (pills)."

> "The other night, I walked home, and a group of boys made me do stuff I did not want to do."

> "I am so sad because I feel so ugly and alone, and I have no friends. All the other girls in my class are skinny, beautiful, and trendy. They make fun of me, but my parents do not know."

> "My parents want me to do gymnasium, but I would like to become a car mechanic. I am afraid to disappoint them."

"I would like to quit my athletic career because now I have a girlfriend. I love her very much and want to spend time with her. I am afraid to tell my parents because they invested so much time and money in my athletic career." (a teen who came in for bedwetting)

"You won't tell my mom, right? Because, you know, I still make myself throw up."

"You won't tell my parents, right? Because, you know, my mom is a doctor, and I smoke pot with my friends."

"You know, I tell my parents that I sleep over at my friend's house, but actually I sleep over at my boyfriend's. I am scared they won't like him because . . ."

"I am supposed to go onto the summer camp, but I feel so homesick. I am ashamed to tell anyone, so I pretend that I am ill."

Do you notice how many teen issues have to do with fear of disappointing the parents? This is why parents need to wait outside. Let me assure you, even if parents call me after the session to ask what the problem was—which is super rare—I do not leak any confidential info to them. Why? Because if the teen finds out, I will never see him again! Twice I have had teen girls who spoke about their suicidal thoughts. All my alarm signals went off. I explained to the teen that, after the session, we would need to look at this with the parents. Both girls agreed, and we looked at it after the session.

In the Pretalk with the parents, **I speak a lot.**

In the Pretalk alone with the teen, **I listen a lot.**

Please do not get the impression that, when working with teens, you only get to work with really tough problems. Not at all! Very often, it is simple issues like:

- Test anxiety
- Heartache
- Lack of self-esteem
- Stuttering
- Bedwetting
- Nail biting
- Nightmares
- All sort of different phobias
- Improving school performance
- Improving sports performance, etc.

I only started working with the more challenging issues, such as those cited earlier, after several of practice, experience, and additional professional training. After I attended studies on hypnosis and psychosis, I felt ready to welcome teens with more serious issues. If you are not yet properly trained or do not feel comfortable with certain issues like self-mutilation, eating disorders, and depression, refer your teen client to a colleague you trust and who is well-trained for it. We have a great responsibility and must stand up for it fully.

Oh, let me share one last very cool door-opener for your pre-talk alone with the teen! Ask the teen about their tattoos because every tattoo has a story that goes with it.

*We have a great responsibility
and must stand up for it fully.*

Since the topic here is the Educational Pre-talk, I will not dive into how I facilitate the actual session with the teen. However, it always involves regression. This is because regression provides me with the best results in a very short time. But before I say "au revoir" to you, dear reader, let me tell you what the ISE was with my teen girl who wet the tissue with tears and mascara.

Finding the ISE

We regressed into the womb of her mom, where she already felt unwanted and unwelcome. The hypnoanalysis involved Chair Therapy with Mom, Dad, and one of her former best friends. Interestingly, this teen girl was the result of artificial insemination. At the ISE, she cried a lot because she had no siblings. (Her mom had lost two embryos before she was born.) In the post-hypnotic interview, she was strongly impressed by this emotion that had come up. It had never crossed her Conscious Mind ever before.

Of course, self-forgiveness was an important part of the process. Then, Future Pacing was used to ensure that she could no longer call forth the original negative emotion she had brought into my office that morning. The feeling that needed to be released was sadness because her dad had received a diagnosis of Amyotrophic Lateral Sclerosis (ALS). This morning, this girl walked out of my office after two hours with a big smile and her eyes full of gratitude.

First sessions with adults usually take me three to three-and-a-half hours, but a teen's subconscious mind is still like wet cement. As a result, sessions are shorter. Working with teens requires less energy because they have not had the time to carve these limiting thoughts and feelings deeply into their subconscious minds. They get the hang of the regression very quickly, and Forgiveness Work is much easier.

While I also work with more minor children and many adults, let me tell you a secret. To HEAL TEENS is what makes me the happiest.

"Au revoir" is not "goodbye," do you agree? It means our paths shall cross again. If it is because I managed to hand over to that bright, shining torch for teen hypnotherapy, it would mean the world to me. If that talented, passionate, and dynamic part inside of you cheered while reading my words here, today, then perhaps you also feel, "Yes, I want to join Barbara and heal teens as well!"

Barbara Scholl

OMNI and HypnoKids® Instructor
barbara.scholl@omnihypnosis.com
https://barbarascholl.com/en/omni-hypnosis-training/
Facebook: hypnokids.net

Every symptom is the result of a life experience. This is the fundamental basis of regression-to-cause hypnosis. ~ **The Devil's Therapy**

CHAPTER 10:
The Science of Hypnotism

Scott Allerton, Australia

W e've all had them . . . those clients that just seem to resist all efforts to gain the common ground where the magic happens. But maybe that's the problem. Maybe we could benefit from "Demystifying Hypnosis" for the client. For me, having the essential foundation of learning is imperative to be in a position to provide sufficient care for the client. This begins with researching their past to understand their present state. That is what I would like to speak to here. I hope my words will be met with curiosity and an open mind.

The first session is the most important in terms of establishing rapport. Part of being able to do that is by putting on your interpersonal glasses and assessing the client's position. When we consider things like early childhood attachment, adverse childhood events, and interpersonal circumstances that lead to adult narratives, it's clear to see why some people can be more resistant than others. This is why it is so important to give the client a thorough understanding of hypnotherapy before taking the next step into therapy.

We all have the natural faculty to be analytical and critical of information that is offered to us. This basic survival mechanism is strong and predominant for self-preservation in humans. It's my clinical experience that it is imperative to provide evidence-based support for the client's ability to make an informed decision if the therapy is right for them. One of the main reasons my clients experience good outcomes is because I take the time to explain the science. Every one of my clients gets the science. This means I don't really have to adapt my pre-talk to suit them individually. As many of my clients already have a higher level of knowledge, I can use more technical terminology. With me, they get a clear explanation of how they got here and what we need to do together to get them where they want to be.

Demystifying Hypnosis

I have spent a lot of time researching the origin and lineage of Hypnotism. As a result, I hold a very scientific view as opposed to a mystical one. The purpose of writing my book, *Demystifying Hypnosis: Where it Originated, Where it Went Wrong, and Where to Go from Here,*[19] was to educate and inspire by sharing what took twenty-five years for the pieces to all fall into place for me.

In fact, I found that there was a person who went to great lengths to remove the mystical element from Mesmerism and animal magnetism of the time in favor of creating a new scientific framework utilizing our natural psychological ability to respond to suggestion. Hénin de Cuvillers, resident member and secretary of the Society of Animal Magnetism, new resident member of the Academic Society Sciences and member of the Society of Sciences and Art in Nantes from the

---

[19] https://www.demystifyinghypnosis.com.au/

Galvanic Society, etc., fiercely opposed Mesmer's claims of possessing a magnetic fluid which he used to turn his patients into puppets, acting at his will. Instead, de Cuvillers offered his insight that the interpersonal rapport or, as he called it, "getting in touch" was the mechanical driver that initiated phenomenological responses in another. De Cuvillers made his formal application to the French academy of science in 1821, complete with nomenclature to support his new scientific theoretical framework, for acceptance in the scientific and medical arena.

There are many different modalities within the suggestive therapeutic field that still incorrectly use the "hypno" terms de Cuvillers coined to describe conditions around transitional light sleep. I am privy to those responsible and why some continue to use terms that describe sleep to describe working states that are fully conscious. I choose to stay firmly grounded in the original framework of Hypnotism, which was created to differentiate the work of the mystics from the psychological science. My views may not be for everyone, and many idols and their followers are quite happy with their chosen suggestive therapy. There are the academics that research, those who are happy to apply the therapy, and some that enjoy both.

Getting in Touch

It is of the utmost importance to present the hypnosis so that the client understands that it is in no way a threat to them. Present it as a threat, and the analytical/critical cortex will come online, putting the client into survival mode. Clients in survival mode are extremely resistant to the process, the psychotherapy, and the suggestions that follow.

When informing the client of what hypnosis is, I use the term quite literally, as it was originally coined, to indicate a set of phenomena found in a subject that participates in the framework of hypnotherapy intending to assist the client in achieving a "working" state of heightened suggestibility.[20] This definition, however, is quite technical for the lay client to understand. Instead, I simply say that, with their permission, I would like to help the client achieve a working-state that is going to increase their ability to respond to suggestions, that this working state is 100 percent natural, and that we will just be utilizing their natural abilities to accept therapeutic suggestions with increased learning efficacy.

The pressure we place on the client to achieve a certain state sets them up to fail, as it becomes their conscious goal to achieve that working state. This is exactly the opposite of what we want to be happening. In addition, while trying to achieve hypnosis, the client may become critical and analytical. Explain to the client that "if we are conscious, we can be conditioned and learn" and that, while everyone can be hypnotized, some may be more resistant than others, which can be helpful. This leaves the client receptive rather than conscious and doubtful that they may not benefit from the session. Even if they aren't as absorbed as they would like to be their first time in the chair, it doesn't really matter because they can accept the therapy as long as they have a level of conscious awareness. "Conscious awareness" in this context means that the cortex (the conscious part of the brain) is active to a degree, even while in stage one, light sleep of Hypnagogia.[21]

---

[20] Please note that when I use the term "state" I am not "naming hypnosis a state,", but merely using it in a descriptive context to indicate the associated phenomena, which is academically acceptable (Hilgard 1969). I will also hyphenate terms to modify the meaning so that I'm not mistaken as subscribing to the more mystical theories of hypnosis being a psychological state/condition.

[21] Hypnagogia, also referred to as "hypnagogic hallucinations." is the experience of the transitional state from wakefulness to sleep: the hypnagogic state of consciousness, during the onset of sleep. (Wikipedia)

Hypnagogia shares many phenomena similar to the working-state achieved in original Hypnotism, with extreme responsivity to suggestion being one of them.

Hypnagogia is said to show a variable 50 percent decreased level of cortical activity as we transition to sleep. Hence the critical and analytical faculty is somewhat suppressed. The more the client gets comfortable with you and your setting, the less active the cortex will become, allowing suggestions to be more readily accepted. It's not essential to aim for a calm, relaxed, semi-sleepy working state of hypnosis, but for me, that is the aim and why I choose to use this approach when appropriate for the individual client. Other suggestive modalities utilize fully conscious working-states, through to active working-states while riding exercise bikes, etc. I see no reason why hypnotic terms that imply transitional sleep should be used to identify these suggestive alert modalities when other more appropriate modern terms can correctly be applied. Correct use of terminology would go a long way to clarifying and differentiating the many varied approaches within the suggestive therapeutics field. The debate over what hypnosis is may just come to an end when the true etymology of the terms and the intention of the scientific framework is known by all.

Assessing the Client

Assessing the client is an important first step toward "getting in touch" with the client and being able to tell how they may respond to the hypnotic process. If a client presents with an extremely high-stress baseline, they can sometimes find themselves with an implicit stress response, which makes them alert and in an unproductive survival state. On the other hand, if the client is sleep-deprived and likely to fall to sleep easily, you may choose an alert approach with them.

Ninety-nine percent of my clients present with stress-related disorders, so my initial intake is thorough and great for assessing analytical clients. Coregulation is important, and I always give my clients a way to regulate themselves should they get an amygdala-mediated stress response. For example, I use mindful breathing at the beginning of the induction. Then, if I see any signs of stress, I can direct the client back to the breath. This teaches the client how to self-regulate while giving the amygdala a chance to regain its composure while the body clears the stress chemicals.

Stephen Porges' Polyvagal Theory is an essential foundation of my clinical practice. I highly recommend that you look this up as many of the conditions which clients present with are based on stress. Polyvagal Theory highlights the fact that the amount of stress in a client's life can determine their baseline level of arousal and, in turn, how they respond to stimuli. I believe that the amount of stress is proportionate to the way we react to stressful stimuli. We primarily respond in three ways; with anger, fear or distress, so the higher our stress baseline, the higher the level of reactivity will be, by either getting angry, fearful, or shutting down. Classic fight, flight, flee, right?

A client with a high-stress baseline generally has a higher amount of stress chemicals in the blood. This includes adrenaline, noradrenaline, and cortisol, which are stress chemicals to increase our alertness so we can deal with threats. If you understand the workings of the amygdala and its role in initiating this stress response to deal with a threat, you may appreciate this. If not, books or videos of Joseph Ledoux will see you in the best hands.

If we don't inform our clients that hypnotherapy or clinical hypnosis is 100 percent safe, they will most likely quickly enter "survival mode," and there will be no calm, receptive working state within them. While we don't always have to aim for transitional sleepy hypnosis, we may want a level of calmness that allows the client to be engaged or "in touch" with us and not preoccupied with a perceived threat. I've found that clients who are in survival-mode can be some of the most resistant. Not knowing about a threat can be as big a threat as knowing about one, so be sure to ask the client if there is anything they are concerned about.

All clients have concerns one way or another. Some are afraid that they will talk and share a secret. Some are afraid that I will make them do things. Others are afraid that they will not come out of hypnosis. It's always good practice to cover all possible myths before beginning the process. This will allow you to limit cortical (conscious) arousal and thus prevent the client from becoming overly analytical. When we are experiencing a stress response, the cortex becomes less active to give more control to the survival parts of our brain. As a result, learning and memory may be inhibited. (This is another great reason to employ the calmest working-state possible, where appropriate.)

Identifying Resistant Clients

Anyone familiar with the work of Daniel Siegel will understand that resistant clients can often have a very narrow window of tolerance. I like to use a freeway to describe this analogy. For example,

> "Imagine yourself driving on a three-lane freeway in the middle lane. You are driving peacefully when a car breaks down in your lane. Well, you have a lane on either side of you, so it's all good.

> "You can be patient and go into the left lane, or you could be tolerant and choose the right. Either way, you have plenty of room within the freeway's barriers to remain calm and deal with

the stress. Having three lanes to maneuver around and avoid stress is your window of tolerance.

"So, you chose the left lane of Patience to get around the broken-down car. And now that lane ends, and you have lost all patience. So, you shoot off to the middle, and the cars are going too slow. So, you cross into the right lane of Tolerance, and it ends also. So, now you have lost all tolerance. You're getting frustrated now, forced back to the middle lane. And then the traffic slows to a stop.

"You have no lane to the left as patience is gone, nor do you have a lane to the right as tolerance has gone too. So, now you're in the single lane of Frustrated/survival mode with only the barriers on each side of you. When someone runs into the back of you, it's the final straw! You are 'shifted' into one of the barriers. Both barriers can be viewed as 'survival states' and, in some cases, coping mechanisms. We can name these survival states, with the right barrier being 'Chaos' and the left being 'Rigidity.'"

There can be many reasons why clients are predisposed to a predominant survival state, including early childhood attachment, adverse childhood events, developmental trauma, and traumatic experiences not necessarily rooted in childhood. Depending on your type of practice and level of training, understanding the client's history is a sure step toward being in a position to effect therapy.

Right-Shifted Clients

Those that are "right shifted" to the barrier of "Chaos" may present in the following ways:

- Anger or distress
- Fear or anxiety
- Intrusive thoughts
- Worry or ruminations
- Hyper-vigilance
- Preoccupied easily
- Distracted

At this stage, we are looking for signs that may indicate that the client is right-hemispheric dominant in a survival state of chaos. If the client is excessively distracted by their intrusive thoughts, preoccupied with other matters, avoiding particular things, or showing a high level of fear or anxiety around the process, these need to be considered before going forward.

Neuroscientists relate the right barrier of chaos to the right hemisphere of our brain, which is highly visual, imaginative, creative, and intimately connected, via the insula cortex, to the emotional limbic part of the brain, where the amygdala and other implicitly involved areas reside. Those that present in a state of Chaos may signal you to explore a possible "anxious ambivalent" early childhood attachment style rendering them preoccupied. For those NLP folks, this client may be more open to visual and kinesthetic learning.

Left-shifted clients

Those that are "left shifted" to the barrier of "Rigidity" may present in the following ways:

- Stubborn
- Inflexible
- Hardened

- Obsessive focus
- Dissociation
- Excessive independence
- Hypo-vigilance
- Lack of empathy

Once again, we're looking for signs that may indicate that the client is left-hemispheric dominant or left shifted to a survival state of Rigidity. Considering the above, I'm sure you may relate these attributes to one particular person in your life who fits the profile. Neuroscientists relate the left barrier of rigidity to the left hemisphere of our brain, which is highly analytical, critical, logical, linear, and linguistic. In short, left-shifted clients may be predisposed to being analytical and critical.

The left-shifted client may be oppositional, defiant, and resistant, which is never a good way to start a hypnotherapy session. This could be due to an "anxious-avoidant" attachment style rendering the adult very dismissive. For those using NLP, this client may be more open to auditory learning. Left-shifted clients can be resistant due to employing a psychological mechanism to cope with a threat due to past trauma.

Have you ever had someone hurt you to the point that you put up a wall? "I'll never let them hurt me again" or "That person has done it, now I'll never trust them." We can view that metaphorical wall as being between both hemispheres, where the logical left hemisphere can create a kind of dissociation toward the emotional limbic region of the right hemisphere. I mentioned earlier that the emotionally survival-driven limbic part of the brain where the amygdala resides is the same area where memories of past trauma and hurt are consolidated and stored. Implicit emotions and feelings are constantly being directed from the bottom up to our conscious awareness to remind us of what possible dangers we should avoid.

In his book, *Mindsight: The New Science of Personal Transformation*, Siegel highlights a pathway linking the body proper to the left hemisphere. This pathway which travels both from the bottom up and from the top down is referred to when discussing vertical integration. Siegel explains that the wisdom of the body comes up the Vagus Nerve, up Lamina I in the spinal cord, and makes stopovers in the limbic/hypothalamic regulatory areas. These regulatory areas concerned with self-preservation emerge up into the middle prefrontal cortex regions of the anterior cingulate cortex and insula, primarily on the right hemisphere of the brain. The right side of the brain is connected to the left by the corpus callosum, which is basically a data cable transferring information between the two hemispheres. The corpus callosum could be viewed as a metaphorical wall separating the left-shifted client's conscious awareness from the negative cautionary feelings and sensations coming up from the right hemispheric limbic area.

This could be considered a coping mechanism that renders left hemispheric-dominant clients resistant to quieting the activity of the left hemisphere. To quiet the left hemisphere is to let down the wall and put the client's conscious awareness in touch with the negative arousal from the right. This may upset the client's emotional homeostatic balance. For those who take an Internal Family Systems perspective (parts), hypnosis could suppress the manager, exposing the protector to the exiled child part causing distress, which the client is trying to avoid. This is another great reason to consider the individual needs of the client before choosing either the calming "original" approach of Clinical Hypnosis/Hypnotism or the "modern" awake/alert, more conscious suggestive approaches such as NLP.

The Best Way to Work with Analytical Clients

There are many different types of suggestive inductions, some are hypnotically sleepy, some are more awake, and others are very active. When working with excessively left-shifted analytical clients, give them something to think about. It can be unproductive to give them suggestions like, "You are relaxed, your mind is clear, there is no tension in your body, etc." because their conscious cortex will start pointing out that you have no idea what they are experiencing. If you do choose the calmer transitional Stage 1 of the Sleep working state, use their own natural interoceptive bodily awareness to increase activation of their right hemisphere. For example,

> Invite your client to notice the cool sensations in their nose as they breathe in, replaced with a warmth on the breath out.

> Invite them to let all the muscles in their eyelids relax. Inform them that when their eyelids close, the light is blocked off, which allows the pineal gland to secrete the sleepy melatonin that can help them to drift down to a semi-sleepy space.

> The more they let their eyelids relax, gravity takes over, and they can become heavier. Then, invite your client to move that relaxed heaviness around their body. This will reduce left hemispheric dominance and increase balance and homeostasis with the right.

Your highly analytical left-shifted client may be more likely to accept your invitations, and before they know it, they will be back in the room, ready to come back for more.

I have given examples of how I apply such psychotherapeutic approaches of Clinical Hypnosis, Neuro-Linguistic Programming, Polyvagal Theory, Interpersonal Neurobiology, Internal Family Systems to gain rapport or "get in touch" with my clients while educating them to observe the issues that highlight the therapeutic way forward.

I learned early on that "the more you learn, the less you know," which becomes my motto more each day. Understanding neuroscientific principles and varied psychotherapeutic approaches helped me develop a somewhat expansive perspective within the suggestive therapeutics field that lacks clarity. Considering that most of my clients present with stress-related dis-order/dis-ease, increasing my knowledge of mind-body connectedness, key brain areas, neural circuitry, and associated biochemistry has been instrumental in assisting my clients to achieve their health goals. It's this kind of client outcome that brings those referrals and reviews that all complement the satisfaction we get by serving the community and being at the front line of shaping a future free of suffering.

I average reading one book per month based on neuroscience, psychology, or psychotherapy. Although the contents are repetitive at times, another piece of the puzzle always seems to fall into place when the author explains something in their unique way. Stepping outside of our expert's mind, which inhibits learning, is a sure first step to being one of those who can benefit when the affectionately labeled "Psychobabble" becomes the bridge to a perspective that supports your growth as a suggestive therapeutic's practitioner.

Whether your approach is Return-to-Cause Hypnosis (R2CH), Original Hypnotism/Clinical Hypnosis, or any of the new breed of modern alert-suggestive therapies, I hope this short chapter acts as such a bridge for you.

Scott Allerton

Clinical Hypnotherapist, holding an advanced diploma in Clinical Hypnosis and Psychotherapy, certification in Neuro-Linguistic Programming (NLP), Mindfulness stress reduction/meditation, Eye Movement Desensitisation Reprocessing (EMDR), Fatigue Management Consultant, and Reiki Master Practitioner.

Sydney Integrative Hypnotherapy
www.SydneyIntegrativeHypnotherapy.com.au
+61 425 297 260

CHAPTER 11:
Hypnotherapy for a Better Death

Daniel Ghanimé

Every one of us has experienced a loss in our life; a father, a friend, a mother, a son, a daughter, a colleague, a neighbor, a classmate, or a life partner. People die on the street, in a hospital, or in their bed. You might meet someone at a bar and, after having a couple of drinks, learn that they've just found out they have terminal cancer. There's never enough experience to cover everyone's situation. And yet, you have your empathy and your care.

> *"He lives badly who does not know how to die well."*[22] ~ **Seneca**

In this chapter, we will not go into an extensive discussion about death. Rather, we will look at how to set up your hypnotherapy session to face death with dignity and respect. Looking at death from the Stoics' point of view will shed light on the importance of Death as a continuum of life rather than the "Dead."

---

[22] Seneca, *How to Die: An Ancient Guide to the End of Life.*

The Client

A dying person is like a child lost at a shopping mall—scared, confused, emotionally numb. They are squeezing out their last drop of willpower to stay strong. They don't want to appear weak in front of everyone they know. They're trying to be a war hero, the family's superhuman, or an unbreakable Hercules. At that moment, when you stand in front of this person, you must see beyond the sickness and vulnerability. You need to see the story that made the client a hero when everyone else is seeing a zero.

Be a good listener to what they will say. If they can't say anything, listen with your eyes. We all know techniques and scripts. But remember that you are in the presence of death. Death is seen as something terrible. It is seen as the enemy. Something the martial arts can teach us is to respect our opponent. Respect Death and be humble in its presence.

As hypnotherapists, we know that the Contract and rapport are established during pre-talk. With terminal cases, you must give 110 percent to establishing trust. After all, the client will be telling you things that they have never told anyone before. You might be the last person they ever see. While this might seem to put a lot of pressure on you, know that the client can emerge from their session feeling ready to cross over and trusting that they will pass away with a smile. And you can feel proud in the knowledge that you gave a human soul a golden ticket to peace and love.

Anyone with a terminal illness or on their deathbed needs comfort and assurance, but it's different for each client. According to Seneca, each time they have an episode, an attack, a severe discomfort, or a near-death experience, they experience what Greek doctors called *meditatio mortis*, "rehearsal for death." Like people who have suffered war traumas, a person with a terminal illness has rehearsed death many times. While billions of pages have been written about death, very few are about how to die. Religions and philosophers have approached death with respect, but the majority show respect for the dead rather than death itself. As a result, even when a person has studied death and practiced death, there remains a fine threat of something missing. That something is respecting death and not fearing death.

> *"There's only one way we can say that the life we*
> *live is long: if it's enough."*[23] ~ **Seneca**

Facing Death

If you think that your client is the only one facing the challenging and frightening experience of death, think again. As a hypnotherapist, trained and practicing the art of making life better for your clients, facing death will put you in a very challenging yet rewarding experience like no other.

Hypnotherapy has been used for thousands of years for healing psychosomatic ailments and mind-related matters. The power of suggestion can be used to evoke regression to the root cause of problems or to progress to visualize success and face future challenges such as test anxiety or battlefield combat. Hypnotherapy can be used to support clients in facing the end of life by:

- Resolving past traumas
- Healing the broken heart and relationship problems
- Restructuring broken family

---

[23] Seneca, *How to Die: An Ancient Guide to the End of Life.*

- Resolving the hero-to-zero feeling
- Completing unfinished affairs and bucket lists, past, present, and future
- Resolving old conflicts, disappointments, and losses
- Dealing with shame, anger, grudge, guilt, and inner pain
- Managing severe stress and anxiety of facing death
- Lessening or relieving unrelieved physical discomfort and pain
- Dealing with the loneliness of dying alone
- Accepting or allowing dependency of others and on others
- Dealing with irregular sleeping patterns and insomnia
- Coming to terms with losing physical functions
- Complementing self-care, being able to accept medication and advice
- Releasing or resolving fear of the unknown and feeling helpless
- Supporting and helping the caregivers of the dying one
- Regaining and fostering peace of mind and accepting death

"A whole lifetime is needed to learn how to live, and—perhaps you'll find this more surprising—a whole lifetime is needed to learn how to die.[24]

~ **Seneca.**

No matter how many people tell you that professional caregiving will give you thicker skin, rest assured that, as a hypnotherapist with a mind-to-mind connection, these people will become a part of your life. Despite their pain, what you can help them achieve is healing from old wounds and the opportunity to fix what they didn't have time to fix. But to hold someone's hand on that journey requires a certain level of

[24] Seneca, *How to Die: An Ancient Guide to the End of Life..*

emotional intelligence. You need to prepare yourself for it. You're going to be handling an angry, frightened, insecure, sad, frustrated, and lonely person who has lost most of their privileges in life. Realize that they are already grieving what they once were. Search within yourself and ask, "Am I the one for this client? Will I be able to handle it well?"

The Cycle of Grief

Elisabeth Kübler-Ross, a Swiss psychiatrist, first introduced her five-stage grief model in her book, *On Death and Dying.* The model was based on her work with terminally ill patients and has received much criticism since. This is mainly because the people studying her model mistakenly believed that this is the specific order in which people grieve and that all people go through all stages.[25]

To help you become familiar with the grieving model, I will list the five phases here, hoping that you will not fall into the same trap of linearity as most.

- Denial
- Anger
- Bargaining
- Depression
- Acceptance

Kübler-Ross now notes that these stages are not linear, and some people may not experience any of them. Others might only undergo two stages, rather than all five, one stage, three stages, etc. It is now more readily recognized that these five stages of grief are the most

---

[25] *The Five Stages of Grief, An Examination of the Kubler-Ross Model,* Christina Gregory, PhD.

observed experienced by the grieving population. In addition, "Bargaining" can present in all the other phases as people tend to find a conscious, rational, analytical, and logical explanation and solution while looking at several "what if" scenarios.

Since the rest of the phases are almost self-explanatory, Bargaining is one of the phases that people ask about the most.[26] What is bargaining?

Bargaining

When something bad happens, have you ever caught yourself making a deal with God? For example, "Please God, if you heal my husband, I will strive to be the best wife I can ever be and never complain again." This is bargaining. In a way, this stage is false hope. You might falsely make yourself believe that you can avoid grief through a type of negotiation. i.e., "If you change this, I'll change that." You are so desperate to get your life back to how it was before the grief event that you are willing to make a major life change in an attempt toward normality.

Guilt is a common wingman of bargaining. This is when you endure the endless "what if" statements. "What if I had left the house five minutes sooner? The accident would have never happened!" "What if I encouraged him to go to the doctor six months ago like I first thought? The cancer could have been found sooner, and he could have been saved!"

---

[26] *The Five Stages of Grief, An Examination of the Kubler-Ross Model, Christina Gregory, PhD.* https://www.psycom.net/depression.central.grief.html

While grief may manifest psychologically, one cannot deny that physical and spiritual manifestations of grief are also equally important. For example, some of the most important signs of grief include:

- Crying
- Headaches
- Difficulty sleeping
- Questioning the purpose of life
- Questioning spiritual beliefs (e.g., belief in God)
- Feelings of detachment
- Isolation from friends and family
- Abnormal behavior
- Worry
- Anxiety
- Frustration
- Guilt
- Fatigue
- Anger
- Loss of appetite
- Aches and pains
- Stress

Challenges

One of the biggest challenges of using hypnotherapy in relation to death is understanding where your patient is standing. Is it upon their request? Is it their family's request? Is it the medical care team's request as part of the treatment? How spiritual or religious they were, they are still, or they've never been? What is their age versus their life experience? Child, adolescent, teenager, adult, or an old person? What is their understanding of death? What is their experience with death? What is their Physical status? Weak, frail, fragile, or strong?

Your approach will depend on whether you are working at your office or in a hospital as part of the palliative care team. Old age, death, and terminal illness are quite different in terms of approach. In addition, you may be facing several barriers when introducing hypnotherapy. Below is a list of the most important obstacles.

Religious System

Many religions oppose hypnotherapy or the idea of pain relief. Some people consider suffering a part of their purification process, a sort of purgatory on earth, and that by suffering, they are bearing their cross. In the Christian last confession in the Church's Sacrament of Anointing of the Sick, the rites are three sacraments combined. First, the believer gives their final confession, and the priest forgives them for their sins. Then, they are anointed by the priest with Holy Water. Finally, the priest performs the Eucharist or the remembrance of the Body and Blood of Christ.

As you can see, forgiveness and guilt-freeing will get people closer to peace and love. The process of coming to forgiveness can happen in whatever way the client requires to enhance the quality of life while facing death. In this case, knowing the client's religious history can support your therapeutic approach. For example, forgiveness work during the session could be executed by an imagined priest. Facilitating the process could also be a joint effort between several people— Physical, Spiritual, and Mental.

Social System

Society has played a major role in putting unnecessary fears on clients. False information, misperceptions, and misconceptions about hypnotherapy only amplify the client's fear of death.

To be labeled as crazy for turning to charlatan stuff at the end of their lives only increases the level of doubt about the effectiveness of hypnotherapy.

Family System

Everyone wants the best for their relative (most of the time), but you might be facing a lot of pressure from family members. As dark as it may seem, some family members may wish to hasten the relative's end of life because of financial situations or heritage.

Educating your client and family members is of the essence. Remember, everyone in the family is facing the fact that death is imminent. They are facing the bitterness of death and entering their own cycle of grief. You will doubtless be faced with many suggestions on how to do your work, which will make it Mission Impossible. A family member dealing with anger may turn to blaming you, suggesting that it's your fault that the person died prematurely, as if anyone has power over death. Know that the people around your client will need therapy, too. Therefore, your utmost understanding and respect for everyone involved will be required.

Legal Issues

Remember that the road to hell is paved with good intentions, and the law doesn't protect the ignorant. There will always be a way to sue someone for malpractice or for using the term "therapy" in a country or state where it is not allowed outside of the medical field. Make sure to do your homework to ensure that your sessions are legally well-covered on all levels.

Belief System

The client's Belief System (BS) is your friend and foe. Sometimes you will find yourself in a situation where each step forward is followed by two steps backward. Make sure to use this to your own advantage by not going against the client's BS until they are ready. Otherwise, you will have the risk of losing rapport. Remember, it is always about your client and not about you.

Medical Professionals

Whether you are recommended by the client's doctor or a family member or friend, make sure to get a signed consent form from the client. Inform the client that their insurance may not offer coverage for your services.

The mind-body relationship is nothing new. Even though Hippocrates recognized it, the lads in white coats are generally not fond of it. As a result, you might find yourself evicted from the room by medical personnel. To avoid this, make sure to do your homework ahead of time by checking with sources of referrals. This is especially important if you are not considered part of the palliative care team.

It doesn't matter how skilled you are. Your closest encounter with medical professionals could be a television program like "Grey's Anatomy," "Scrubs" or "The Good Doctor." But it would be intimidating for anyone to try to mingle or blend in with the medical profession's white, blue, and green uniforms or try to be part of their protocols. It is normal not to have all your confidence in place. If you feel terrified wondering about how to talk to a medical professional and what language or vocabulary to use, here's what you need to keep in mind:

You are not supposed to know it all. Don't worry about not knowing much about body parts and medical terms. The medical care team will tell you more than enough about your client. You will find yourself learning everything you need to know to do what you are supposed to do. Your job is to be an integrative part of a complementary therapy designed to make the client's present life and facing their future death as dignified and respected as possible.

Don't be afraid to ask questions. It's better to show eagerness to learn than it is to fake who you are not. Go ahead and ask, "What can you tell me about Mr./Mrs. Smith's case?" Then treat this conversation as part of your first session intake and pretalk. If the team buys in, they will become your allies and make it easier for you to bypass all the previously mentioned barriers.

While it seems like it's all about you making a difference in someone's life, you are also offering a way for the team to cope with their daily stress. Don't shy away from doing what you do best. Remember, behind those white coats, there are humans with many challenges.

> *Know that the same outcome awaits us all, but*
> *dying fearfully, often, is itself a cause of death.*[27]
>
> ~ **Seneca**

Emotional Intelligence in Action

In your practice, you could find yourself stumbling over a greater number of emotionally illiterate people. These clients struggle to understand and manage the basic emotions they are facing, such as

---

[27] Seneca, *How to Die: An Ancient Guide to the End of Life.*

anger, fear, hurt, shame, guilt, grief, and sadness. Understanding these painful emotions will give you a way to start a conversation as part of the process of qualifying your client. You should also know that how you treat yourself will make a major difference in dealing with adversity. After all, no one wants you to crack under pressure, suffer emotional drainage, or burnout. Make sure you know how to identify what you are feeling and how to manage your own emotional states.

Many people don't know the difference between sacrifice and compromise. To them, it feels like they mean the same thing. This is also true of words like sympathy, empathy, and compassion. Sympathy means feeling sorry for your client but not feeling their suffering. Empathy means putting yourself in their shoes, feeling and experiencing their pain and suffering to a certain extent. Compassion means rising above empathy to take action by offering help while feeling with them.

It is never easy to go through the death experience. To offer the best assistance to a dying patient, you must become comfortable with your own mortality. You are, after all, a finite human. One day, you will eventually die. You need to get comfortable talking about death and let your authentic emotions guide you rather than blocking you. Always remember that it's about the client; it's not about you. Getting emotional and telling your own story isn't helpful. Most of the time, it's counterproductive. Your experiences don't matter to the client. It is not *you* who is facing death; it's the client. You are not obliged to tell your client that you know how they feel because, believe me, you don't.

Some clients may have lived through a near-death experience. Some may have experienced clinical death. But, the finality of death as the result of a terminal disease can only be experienced once by the patient. No matter what age they might be, there's always uncertainty. Of all human fears, fear of the unknown is the most pervasive. Many serious psychologic disorders are based, at least in part, upon the fear of death itself or fear of the experience of dying.[28] A cancer patient, for example, might express significant fear and anxiety over the actual mechanics of their death. These anxieties could include the fear that the experience will be extraordinarily painful, extremely disruptive for the family, or that the client will manifest cowardice during the final stages.

There is a general uneasiness towards death in our society. As a result, the client may experience the fear of rejection, of dying alone and uncomforted during the final hours of life. The therapeutic process should focus on accepting death as a natural conclusion to a biological chain of events. Death should never be perceived as a defeat or a failure.

Preparing for Death

Helping someone to die must clearly be distinguished from the act of causing someone to die. As few patients are familiar with the concept of "helping someone to die," it can be useful to ask the client whether they would like to learn a little about what it is like to die. If the question is posed in a caring way, almost universally, clients will respond affirmatively.

With the client's permission, you can then use the following Death Rehearsal Technique[29] to allow the client to confront their fears and anxieties about dying. A death rehearsal will enable patients to approach their worries, fears, anguish with security, control, and peace

---

[28] Feifel, Freilich & Herman, 1973.
[29] Levitan, A. A. (1985). Hypnotic Death Rehearsal. *American Journal of Clinical Hypnosis*, 27(4), 211–215.

of mind. The patient is often grateful for having shared the death experience with the hypnotherapist and will be comforted knowing that the hypnotherapist is available if required.

> *We must prepare for death before life. Our life is well furnished, yet we're greedy for its furnishing; somethings always seem to be lacking, and always will. It's not years not days, but the mind that determines that we've lived enough.* ~ **Seneca**

Death Rehearsal

Once the client's fears and anxieties have been discussed, a hypnotic trance is induced by whatever method seems mutually acceptable to the therapist and the patient. Ideomotor signals can then be established.

Move the client to a point in the future where death is imminent. Note: this is subjective and may not be related to current physical challenges.

Instruct the client to signal when they have arrived. Then afford the client the ability to speak while remaining in the trance state.

From here, the process is facilitated in the same way as a Regression Hypnotherapy session. Elicit details about the experience, including place, surroundings, etc., identify painful emotions, and guide the client to a peaceful resolution.

Conclusion

When a person asks you, "How to die?" tell them, "Prepare yourself, have no fear, have no regrets, set yourself free, and become part of the whole. And if you need someone to walk you through it, I will be there beside you every step of the way." Hypnotherapy can be used to support clients in facing the end of life by helping them come to peace with both their past and impending death.

The process of helping a person to die begins with listening. Let the client tell you their story. Recognize that you are in the presence of Death. Respect Death and be humble in its presence.

To hold someone's hand on that journey requires a certain level of emotional intelligence. You need to prepare yourself for it. A dying person is grieving what they once were. Search within yourself and ask, "Am I the one for this client? Will I be able to handle it well?"

The challenges to be faced when working with a palliative patient include their religious system, social system, family system, legal issues, beliefs, and medical professionals who are part of their care team. Know that the people around them are also suffering. You can help them, too.

Many people are emotionally illiterate. As a result, they struggle to identify and cope with uncomfortable emotions. It's never easy facing death. You need to be comfortable with your own mortality to be an effective guide for your clients.

Preparing a client for death can help to alleviate the fears and anxieties that naturally arise when a person is facing the end of life. Facilitating a Death Rehearsal gives the client a way to confront their fears and finally come to peace. Know that your client can emerge from their session with you, prepared to meet death with a smile. And you can feel proud in the knowledge that you have given a human soul a beautiful gift of healing.

Daniel Ghanimé MBA, CHT, EIDS.

Morphopsychologist, Clinical Hypnotherapist.
Parenting Coach, Emotional Intelligence Development Specialist
DEHI Hypnoanalysis Trainer
The Control Alternative
+961(0)3348853

CHAPTER 12:
Conclusion

Anything you do to educate a person about what you do and how you can help is essentially a pre-talk. Whether you are marketing your services, booking the first session, or preparing a client to be successful working with you, the purpose of your pre-talk is always to establish a contract. For example, your marketing strategies should educate a prospective client about who you can help, what you can help them with, and how you are uniquely qualified to do that.

The purpose of your marketing pre-talk is to invite a prospective client to learn more by having a conversation with you. That's the Contract—the Call. Your first conversation with a prospective client allows you to qualify your clients. This ensures you are getting the best clients *for you*. You can then educate your new client in a way that prepares them for their first session with you. Booking the first session establishes a contract.

Your first session educational pre-talk is an empowerment process that prepares your client to successfully work with you. Your Mind Model acts as a visual aid that speaks to both the client's Conscious and

Subconscious Mind. However, the pre-talk for Regression Hypnotherapy needs to be more comprehensive than a basic hypnosis pre-talk because Regression Hypnotherapy requires the client's participation. Educating the client about how the Mind works, how hypnosis works, and how you and the client will work together to achieve the client's Therapeutic Goal satisfies the needs of both the Conscious and Subconscious minds.

Making your pre-talk relevant to the client's presenting issue satisfies the Conscious Mind's need for reason and logic. Showing the client why there's nothing wrong with them, that their Subconscious Mind is doing what it was designed to do, can earn you powerful rapport with the client's Subconscious Mind. This helps make it safe for the client to give you permission to guide them into hypnosis and regress them into painful past events.

The Contract for Regression Hypnotherapy defines the Therapeutic Relationship by establishing who does what. All healing is self-healing. The client must be prepared to do the work necessary to heal. This includes reviewing and re-evaluating painful past experiences from a more mature point of view. You are responsible for guiding the process. The client is responsible for the results.

Every symptom of dis-ease has roots in a stressful life experience. The process of revisiting and re-evaluating the stressful situations in the past, which generated the stress response, can transform a person's psychobiology from one of dis-ease to one of health and peace. To accomplish this, the client needs to know that regression does not reveal the truth or facts about what happened. It reveals how an event was experienced at a specific age.

While everyone has unresolved trauma from childhood, trauma is not what most people think. Often, the client's issue is rooted in an event in childhood that was simply misinterpreted. Transforming the thoughts and feelings of the client's Inner Child will change how the client thinks, feels, and responds to situations in daily life now.

Teaching your clients how to work with the Subconscious Mind by keeping the focus on the body can give you a strong Bridge to the causal event. The Subconscious Mind is the feeling Mind. Uncomfortable emotions such as fear, sadness, and anger are felt in targeted areas of the torso—for example, the gut, chest, or throat.

Avoidance of painful memories and emotions is a common problem for many people. Teaching a client how to find, name, and release a feeling to feel better provides proof that it's safe for the client to allow uncomfortable feelings and emotions to be a part of the process. This can give you a more cooperative client to work with.

Tapping is a versatile tool that can be used at every phase of the healing process. When used in Regression Hypnotherapy sessions, tapping can quickly and easily help to release stuck emotions. In addition to being used as a releasing technique, tapping can be used as a:

- Convincer
- Confusional induction
- Bridging technique
- Spontaneous regression
- Homework assignment
- Self-healing strategy

The four Universal Healing steps can be combined with any releasing techniques you might use, including:

- Tapping/rubbing
- Pillow therapy
- Breathwork
- Autosuggestion

Once the client knows how to find, feel, claim and release a feeling to feel better, you can teach the client how to test for the ISE by recognizing when a feeling is new or familiar.

The three Fs in the Contract establish a clearly defined Therapeutic Contract that allows both hypnosis and Regression to Cause to happen. The 3-F Exercise gives you a way to test the client's willingness to:

1. **F**ollow instructions
2. **F**ocus on feelings
3. Respond with **F**irst impressions.

You now have a basic framework you can use to create your own pre-talk for Regression Hypnotherapy. The secret to an effective educational pre-talk is:

1. Customize to the needs of the client
2. Consistency in delivery

Your intake provides the information you need to make your pre-talk relevant to each client's specific issues and concerns. If you conduct your intake process first, you'll have everything you need to customize to the client's needs. If you're consistent in delivering a comprehensive educational pre-talk and teach your clients how to work with you before you guide them into hypnosis, you'll have fewer problems to deal with.

Regression gives access to information trapped in the
causal event. Releasing removes the Subconscious
requirement for symptoms.
~ The Devil's Therapy

Working with teenaged clients can be highly rewarding work. But you need to adapt your pre-talk to satisfy your client's needs and the parents of your teenaged client. Barbara Scholl has shared generously, from her wealth of experience, strategies that can help you prepare your teen clients for Regression Hypnotherapy.

Analytical clients can be tough customers. They seem resistant because they have a greater need to understand. Having a basic understanding of neuroscience can support you in customizing your educational pre-talk to the needs of your more analytical clients. Scott Allerton shared a more science-based approach to educating these clients by bridging the fields of neuroscience and psychology/psychotherapy with hypnosis.

Hypnotherapy can support a client in experiencing a better, more peaceful ending of life by relieving common symptoms and preparing the client for death. Daniel Ghanimé revealed the common fears associated with death and dying, challenges that often arise with palliative patients, and how emotional intelligence—your own and the client's—is essential to helping a client come to peace with the ending of life.

The Biggest Challenge

Regardless of who your client might be—highly emotional, emotionally illiterate, analytical, teen or parent—the biggest challenge you're likely to face with your educational pre-talk will be staying consistent. Face it, when you've said it a thousand times before, it's easy to assume you've already covered the pertinent information. You may not even realize you're doing it, but the tendency is to start shortening the pre-talk in an attempt to save time.

When you start skipping over parts of your pre-talk, it can impact your outcomes. As a result, you may find that, over time, you're not getting the same results. You may not realize why this is happening. And when your pre-talk is incomplete, it can also show up in your sessions as client resistance. For example, you begin the uncovering procedure, and the client says, "I can't see anything." (Testing the three Fs in the Contract would have addressed this ahead of time!) Your pre-talk should get rid of unnecessary resistance before you start guiding the client into hypnosis.

The problem is that delivering the same pre-talk, over and over, again, gets boring. Unconsciously, you may start cutting corners. Some hypnosis practitioners try to overcome this problem by recording their educational pre-talk. If the client can watch or listen to the pre-talk before the first session, the rationale is that it will save valuable session time. While this is true, it creates two problems.

First, most people have busy lives. They either won't get around to watching your presentation or, if they do, by the time they show up for their session, they'll have forgotten what it was about.

Second, your educational pre-talk is an integral part of the overall healing process. It helps to lay the foundation for the therapeutic process. To be effective, it needs to be personalized for each client. You can't do that until you have conducted the intake process. A canned presentation is simply too generic to be of much value to anyone.

The Next Step

You have everything you need to create your own pre-talk. The next step is to make a list. Outline the key elements you want to include in your pre-talk. Then, create a PowerPoint presentation you can use to educate your clients in each session. When you complete the intake process, all you need to do is pull out your tablet or laptop and click or swipe through the slides. While you're doing that, you'll be setting the tone for a deeper level of intimacy. That's the Therapeutic Relationship! The Therapeutic Relationship is the foundation for effective hypnotherapy.

Having a pre-build pre-talk presentation will keep you consistent by ensuring that you deliver the same pre-talk to each of your valued clients. All you need to do is customize it to the needs of each client. Simple, right?

Use pictures to illustrate key points. Remember, pictures and images speak to the Subconscious level of Mind. This will make the information more "brain sticky" for both you and the client. Keep the words on the screen to a minimum. The worst thing you can do is fill the screen with text and read it to the client. Most of us have had to sit through this kind of presentation. It's boring. It also gives the impression that you don't know what you're talking about.

Use a few key words to emphasize important concepts. As you guide your client through the presentation, make each key point relevant to the client's issue. Keywords should act as reminders. They remind the client about the point you want to emphasize while reminding you to stay on topic and not get side-tracked.

Your educational pre-talk should be more of a conversation than a presentation. Make it an interactive process. This makes it an engaging learning experience for the client. It holds their attention because everything you're telling the client is about them. It's about how *their* Mind works, how *they* feel, and how following your instructions will help them achieve *their* Therapeutic Goal. Remember, that's what they're paying you for!

Creating an interactive educational pre-talk[30] can support you in establishing a Contract that allows you to deliver the best outcomes possible. As you guide the client through your pre-talk, you can answer questions, teach techniques, test and assess the client's responses. This is how you make the client a partner in their healing.

Radical Healing is the essence of Regression to Cause Therapeutic Hypnosis. To heal means to restore to wholeness. Radical means root. The goal is to restore a person to their natural state of wellbeing— physically, mentally, emotionally, or spiritually—by going upstream of the symptoms to resolve the root cause. That's the Contract.

Thanks for joining me on the healing journey.

Warmly,
Wendie

P.S. If you like what you've got so far, please take a moment to write me a review! It helps others decide to choose that this is a valuable resource for them.

---

[30] You can get a complete done-for-you educational pretalk PowerPoint presentation as part of the Ready for Regression First Session course at www.tribeofhealers.com/ready-for-regression-first-session-system-course/

The Devil's Therapy Series

Book 1: The Devil's Therapy: *Hypnosis Practitioner's Essential Guide to Effective Regression Hypnotherapy*

Book 2: Ditch the Pitch: *Simple Proven Client Attraction Strategies for Hypnosis Practitioners Who Don't Love Digital Marketing*

Book 3: Ditch the Script: *Get Everything You Need from the Client for Successful Hypnotherapy and Set Up to Wrap Up with Results*

Book 4: Radical Healing: *Hypnosis Practitioner's Guide to Harnessing the Healing Power of the Educational Pretalk*

Book 5: The Devil's Little Black Book: *Regression Hypnotherapist's Troubleshooting Guide with Tips, Tricks & Even Scripts to Tweak Your Therapeutic Technique*

Book 6: The Dream Healing Practitioner Guidebook: *A Healer's Guide to Uncovering the Secret Messages of Your Dreams*

Book 7: Ready for Regression: *Hypnosis Practitioner's Guide to Preparing Clients for Effective Regression Hypnotherapy*

Wendie Webber

W|ith over thirty years of experience as a healing practitioner, Wendie brings a broad range of skills to her unique approach to Regression to Cause hypnosis.

She is an Omni-Hypnosis graduate, 5-Path practitioner, Transactional hypnotherapist, Alchemical hypnotherapist, Satir Transformational Systemic therapist, and Regression Hypnotherapy Boot Camp participant.

Before hypnosis, Wendie owned a self-help bookstore where she explored spirituality, psychology, and energy-based healing.

Wendie is the recipient of the 2006 5-PATH Leadership Award and the 2019 Gerald F. Kein OMNI Award for Excellence in Hypnotism.

She enjoys an eclectic lifestyle on Vancouver Island, British Columbia, Canada, surrounded by nature, oracles, and cats. Her courses are available at TribeofHealers.com

The Devil's Therapy: *Hypnosis Practitioner's Essential Guide to Effective Regression Hypnotherapy.* Discover how a 200-year-old fairy tale reveals a complete system for facilitating effective regression hypnotherapy. Learn the "Why" behind the "How-To" of regression to cause hypnosis. Turn your hypnosis sessions into healing programs and get results that last. This practical guidebook gives you a step-by-step map you can use to facilitate successful regression therapy. It's much simpler than you might imagine.

> *This is absolutely amazing work. It's so clear and precise, just like a laser. It leaves no doubts about what to do, how to do it, and the best part: Why to do it!!* - **Zoran Pavlovic, Belgrade, Serbia**

The Devil's Therapy provides a simple three-phase, seven-step protocol for facilitating regression to cause therapeutic hypnosis. The first phase is comprised of three steps which effectively set up for a multi-session healing program. The second phase is comprised of two steps which make up the core work of regression to cause and inner child work. The third phase involves the final two steps of testing/integrating all changes followed by the forgiveness work.

Available on Amazon in English, German, and French versions.

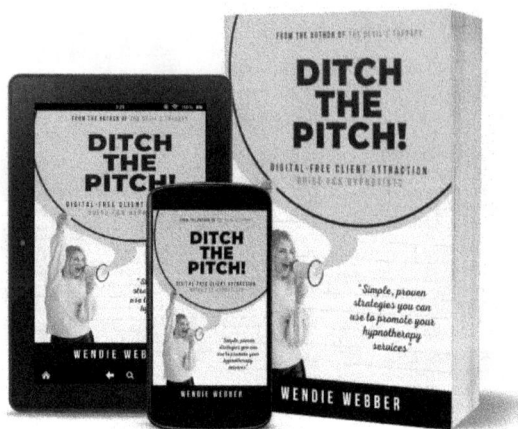

Ditch the Pitch! Digital Free Client Attraction Guide for Hypnotists is a beginner's guide to marketing yourself and your services *without* having to do that dreaded sales pitch, figure out how to game the algorithms on social media, or stay on top of SEO. This is an old-school, hands-on approach for healers who want to take care of business by connecting with real people who truly need your help. That's it.

> *"I've paid a lot of money for business courses and never completed them. I felt overwhelmed and lost in all the content. This course was easy, simple to follow, and taught me so much. I feel confident and ready to change my current system and start implementing what I've learned in my own practice".* – **Nicole D**

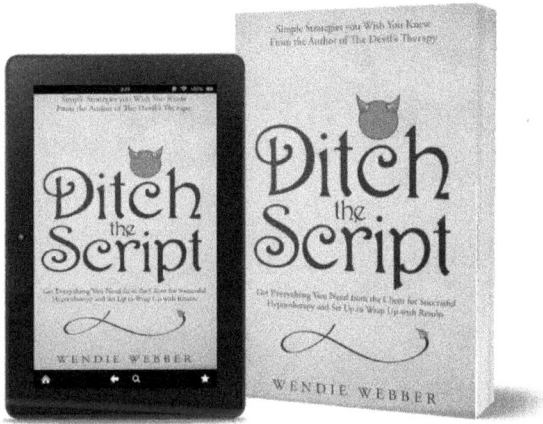

Ditch the Script: *Get Everything You Need from the Client for Successful Hypnotherapy and Set Up to Wrap Up with Results.* Your success is always going to be in your set up. Ditch the Script reveals simple strategies you can use right away to break free of 'scriptnotism' and start facilitating client-centered regression to cause therapeutic hypnosis. Learn how to qualify your clients, conduct the strategic intake process, and more.

I read the first chapter before bed. Wow! Really good! Can't wait to absorb this book!! I didn't think anything could top the first book. After reading one chapter of this second book, I was clearly wrong! – **Michael Madden, USA**

, Australia

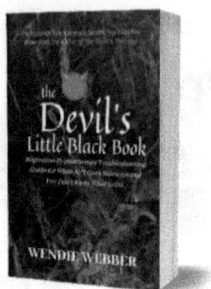

The Devil's Little Black Book: *Regression Hypnotherapist's Troubleshooting Guide with Tips, Tricks & Even Scripts to Tweak Your Therapeutic Technique.* Where *The Devil's Therapy* answers the question, "Why do we do what we do when we do it?" *The Devil's Little Black Book* answers the question, "What if?" What if sh*t happens in a session and you don't know what to do? This companion guide to *The Devil's Therapy* provides proven strategies for dealing with some of the more predictable ways resistance can show up in your sessions with client – and what to do when it does.

After almost 40 years of doing hypnosis, I discovered your phenomenal books and online videos very recently and it opened up the floodgates of memories in my career. Your history of hypnotherapy, your trials and tribulations, parallel mine . . . I am going to recommend your books to all those people who've been bugging me to put to paper these principles. I wish I had heard of you years before when I was active, and an industry turned against me because I refused to take shortcuts and jump on the latest bandwagon of change-work for the month. – **John Petrocelli, USA**

Dream Healing Practitioner Guidebook: *A Healer's Guide to Uncovering the Secret Messages of Your Dreams*. Learn deceptively simple techniques you can use – yourself and with others – to uncover the meaning of your dreams. If you're a healing practitioner, *Dream Healing* gives you an insight therapy you can offer to clients. *Dream Healing* can help you to develop valuable skills that can support you in your healing sessions with clients. Working with your own dreams can help you to develop intuition while bringing balance and harmony to your mind-body system.

Makes Things So Simple

*I have thoroughly loved working with dream healing tools. Wendie makes things so simple and easy that learning new skills such as dream healing become easy to apply and implement from the start. I have absolutely loved uncovering my dream meanings and then putting what I've learnt into action because understanding a dream is not enough; it also needs some change/action for resolution to happen. It's been such an interesting and fun experience. Thank you, so much! – **Nicole Dodd, UK***

Ready for Regression: Hypnosis Practitioner's Guide to Preparing Clients for Effective Regression Hypnotherapy

Ready for Regression: *Hypnosis Practitioner's Guide to Preparing Clients for Effective Regression Hypnotherapy.* The Ready for Regression First Session System is based on a five-star rated course. Gain the confidence you need to guide your clients through the multiple healing processes of Regression to cause therapeutic hypnosis.

IT WORKS!!!! I just finished a NEW session with a NEW client located in Asia. I had my semi-completed session manual with me that I put together based on your training course and . . . wow. It works. Confidence was back. Client felt great. Deep trance. I could go on forever. In short - thank you, Wendie. I put your course and method to real life and IT WORKS!!!!!! It works!!!! A huge suffocating hug to you!!! Thank you!!! And I didn't even complete all the courses yet!!!

~ *Jo Nontakorn*

Get clear. Get confident

www.ingramcontent.com/pod-product-compliance
Lightning Source LLC
Chambersburg PA
CBHW051731020426
42333CB00014B/1263

9 781777 412166